THIRD EDITION – Author's Note
Please read – it's really important!

Over six years have passed since I originally published this story. I can honestly say I have never sat down and re-read the entire book since the final proof was approved. It still hurts too much.

There have also been a lot of significant events in our family since the original publication. Most notably (at least in the context of this story), my husband and I had another daughter almost eighteen months to the day of Stephen's passing. Her name was Esther. She was entirely beautiful. And she was stillborn at thirty-four weeks.

I am still crushed.

A friend once told me that if you shatter a glass vase once, you may be able to put the pieces back together in a way that resembles what it was before. But if you shatter it a second time, good luck to you.

If you have read this book before, you will know that when I lost my son Stephen I went to a very dark place; a place I thought I could never be any darker or hurt any worse than it did. But I held to my faith and everything I believed, and was on the way to significant restoration when I penned the final words.

After we lost Esther and the vase was shattered a second time, I am not ashamed to admit that things fell apart irreparably. I suffered from Post Traumatic Stress Disorder and developed acute clinical anxiety as well as suicidal depression. I also have a chronic illness that I have suffered from since childhood (Fibromyalgia), and I developed new and severely debilitating symptoms. I was trying to be a wife to my husband, a loving mummy to my other beautiful children, and failing miserably at both.

Similarly distressing was the way in which my faith was completely stripped down once again. This time its restoration has been entirely different. I have been forced to closely examine my faith and all it entails and have come to recognise that roughly ninety percent of what I thought was part of a "healthy Christian faith" was in fact cultural; part of a Western Christian culture that was unhelpful at best.

There have been countless times over the past four years I have thought about un-publishing this book and removing it from the shelves. There are authors and preachers I have quoted in these pages whose views I now question. I don't think the same way I used to, and frankly I am embarrassed by my own hubristic, naïve and judgmental attitude.

Yet in spite of all this, there are some basic views expressed in this book that have not changed. I do believe that God loves me. I do believe that he has brought purpose out of Stephen's life and his gut-wrenching death. I do believe that Stephen is in heaven being parented by the most awesome father of all.

It is with that in mind that I ask you to be kind as you read this book. If the theology makes you want to tear your eyes out, you're not the only one. If you are balking at some judgmental remarks and assumptions I've made, I'm right alongside balking at it too.

But it's an honest account of who I was at that time in my life. I have come to learn that it's better to be truthful about how we grow in our faith and how the truth of the gospel can withstand whatever we throw at it.

If you can set aside most of the gag-worthy self-righteous nonsense, there are still many valuable lessons to be learned from Stephen's story. The value of human life. The sacrificial love of a parent. The servant-heart of a spouse. These are the reasons I keep this book on the shelf. My son's life holds deep value and I aim to honour him by sharing his story.

If you're interested in understanding some of what has changed for me, I have since written two more books that provide a narrative to this metamorphosis of faith. They are raw and real, and I hope they might encourage anyone who is wrestling with the idea that their faith cannot withstand the real-life challenges that get thrown their way.

In other news, if you want to learn more about what I am up to these days and the surprising places this journey has taken me, you can visit me at hannahboland.com.au

Other books by this author

I'm Sad and I Need Cake

By Hannah Boland and Cecily Paterson

What do you say when your friend's baby dies? What do you say when her second baby is tragically stillborn? Is there any 'right' way to respond to grief? And when you're the one who's suffering, how do you get through the day? What do you say to the God who could have prevented such tragedy?

Hannah Boland and Cecily Paterson wrote letters to each other for a year, beginning the month after Hannah's second baby's funeral. This candid Christian correspondence is sometimes tragic, sometimes wry and often awkward. But it is always honest, and always looking for the way forward.

Superstitious Christianity

By Hannah Boland with K. Broughton, S. Clancy & J Sharpe

"I know that I love God, but I'm not sure that I like him very much."

After several years of the deepest and most intense emotional suffering, this is how Hannah introduces the themes for *Superstitious Christianity*.

Weighed down by intense grief and feeling disillusioned with the God of the Bible she has faithfully followed, Hannah was faced with a number of difficult questions about her faith - questions that most Christians would shy away from asking.

Determined to rip away the "Superstitious Fluff" of Christianity, Hannah seeks answers from three of her most trusted Christian mentors. The result is what is described as "*an unequalled apologetic that insists the reader returns to the source that Hannah has found – a revelation of God in the midst of suffering!*" (Rev Denis V Smith, Keystone Resources).

Visit hannahboland.com.au/books for more information

The reason apocalyptic and disaster movies are so popular is because we all love to engage in the "What would I do in that situation?" and "How would I cope?" questions. Of course, the good thing about movies is that when you turn them off, you don't have to think about them anymore. They're not real life. But Hannah and Michael's story *is* real life. They really did have to face the "What would I do?" question. And they really had to live the "How would I cope?" answer.

This is a story about a family's gritty, determined, trusting obedience to God, about God's faithfulness and grace, and about a little boy who brought more truth and love with him in his 47 short hours on earth than anyone would have believed possible. It's a story about the complicated and broken nature of real life. And it's a useful reminder to those of us who haven't starred in our own apocalyptic movies as yet to be caring, compassionate and practical in our help to our friends and loved ones who are grappling with problems that seem far, far too big to handle on their own.

Thank you, Hannah, for writing 47 Hours with a Prince.
Cecily Paterson, author of *Love, Tears & Autism*
www.cecilypaterson.squarespace.com

For Stephen and for JC.

47 Hours with a Prince

GOD'S GRACE THROUGH HEARTBREAKING CIRCUMSTANCES

Hannah Boland

47 Hours with a Prince – Third Edition
© Hannah Boland, 2018
First edition published July, 2012
Second edition published December, 2013

This book has been published by the author.
47hourswithaprince.com.au
hannahboland.com.au
hannahboland.com.au/churches

Unless otherwise indicated Scripture quotations are from the *ESV Bible*® (*The Holy Bible, English Standard Version*®), copyright © 2001 by Crossway Bibles, a publishing ministry of Good News Publishers. Used by permission. All rights reserved.

Scripture quotations marked CEV are taken from the Contemporary English Version copyright © 1995 by the American Bible Society, New York, NY. All rights reserved.

Scripture quotations marked AMP are taken from the Amplified Bible, copyright © 1954, 1958, 1962, 1964, 1965, 1987 by The Lockman Foundation. All right reserved.

Scripture quotations marked GNT are taken from Good News Translation, copyright © 1992 by American Bible Society. All rights reserved.

Scripture quotations marked NIV are taken from the New International Version copyright © 1973, 1978, 1984, 2011 by Biblica, Inc. All rights reserved.

(Paperback) ISBN 978-0-646-57687-9
(Kindle) ISBN 978-0-646-57891-0
(ePub) ISBN 978-0-987-5787-0-9

All rights reserved. Except as may be permitted by the Copyright Act, no part of this publication may be reproduced in any form or by any means without prior permission from the author.

Cover design and typesetting by Hannah Boland.
Cover design © Hannah Boland, 2012
Cover artwork by Allison Boland.
Description: The Boland family standing under God's rainbow. From left to right: Daddy, Mummy (holding baby Stephen), Allison & Harry.

Contents

Introduction 1

'Tis the Season to Be Jolly 7

What's in a Name? 19

A Hart of Compassion 33

And Now We Wait 44

A Study in Psalm 139 57

The Wall 68

The Arrival 79

A Servant's Heart 92

Keith Green—the Ministry Years Continue 108

Great Expectations 113

Friend with Benefits 121

A Year of Firsts 128

Head Joy or Heart Joy? 137

Jesus—the Founder and Perfecter of Our Faith 144

Epilogue 149

Acknowledgments

It is difficult to know where to begin when thanking the countless people who have loved and supported me and my family throughout these two journeys—both the journey of pregnancy and grief and my journey of writing this book.

In the former category, I would like to thank all of our friends and family who have gone out of their way to show us love, support, and encouragement during this time of suffering—too many to name. Your thoughts, and more importantly, your prayers, have meant the world to Michael and me. Although it sounds a little silly to say, I actually had a sense of your prayers over us like a warm, spiritual blanket, and I am grateful to have had the prayers of so many saints upon our family. They have indeed been answered.

More specifically, I am thankful for the friends who have hung in there for the long haul—the ones who regularly check up on me and force me out of hiding (in love, of course). To Rachel, Sally, Naomi, and Lesley, the frequent meals on my doorstep, the messages and cards of love and support, and your continued consideration of me and my family have been both overwhelming and deeply appreciated. I know you have all felt so helpless, but how you have served us has been helpful beyond description. To Kirsty and Steve, your friendship, teaching, and prayer have meant more to me than I can express.

To the mother's union at our church, I am continually blown away by the way in which you serve your church and your community, which has included your generosity of time and resources towards our family. The way you served us on the day of Stephen's funeral is something I shall never forget, and I look forward to the time in my life where I may be able to serve others in the way you have served us. Thank you for your faithfulness.

To my sister, Jannah, and my "other sister," Clare, your friendship and support have helped see me through the roughest of days, and it is my continued privilege to share my life with you both.

To my mum and dad, who have spent hours babysitting, doing laundry, cooking meals, praying for us, and loving us the words thank you make my gratefulness seem menial, yet they are the only words I have.

To Cecily Paterson, for the encouragement to keep working on this book, bless you! Reading your story (*Love, Tears & Autism*, 2011) and being so encouraged by God's work in your life and in your family in such a similar way to my own gave me the drive to finish this project in the hope that I might be of encouragement to others. Thank you for all of your advice and guidance and most of all for being an awful sinner like me and being truly un-amazing.

To each of you who read my drafts—Michael, Jannah, Clare, Mary, Marge, Di, and Lynda—I sincerely thank you for your feedback and encouragement, without which this book would never have made it to print.

To Amanda Price, my editor, thank you for turning my split infinitives and other grammatical faux pas into a book that readers can actually understand. Thank you for your encouragement and wisdom, and for persevering through three different computers.

More specifically to Jannah, thank you for all of your research and assistance with the nitty-gritty stuff I despise so much. Thank you for helping me to turn this book into what I hope is a source of clarification and information on certain medical facts that will assist others in their decision making. I have not the brain for it, and I am ever grateful that at least one of us does.

Finally, to my husband, thank you for being my best friend. We have grown together so much throughout this chapter of our lives, and this book is my gift to the both of us. Thank you for being patient with me and loving me through the pregnancy, the grief, and the project. I am truly blessed to have you as my husband and the father of all our beautiful children.

Precious in the sight of the Lord is the death of his saints.

Psalm 116:15

Prince n.
the son of a monarch.[i]

Introduction

On many ways, this book has been a selfish endeavour. All my life I have been increasingly disturbed by the fragility of our own minds. We know things have happened, either to ourselves or to others, but as time goes on (and sometimes only days or months), we begin to question what we saw, thought, felt, or experienced. Did that *really* happen?

Politics thrives on this fragility of the mind. When politicians are forced to make controversial decisions or take action, they usually do it as far away from election time as possible. Our would-be leaders rely on the majority of voters forgetting the deed by the time ballot papers are distributed.

In a similar sense, I have often wondered about the Israelites coming out of Egypt. How could they have been so dense? How could they have possibly forgotten the mighty works of God they had seen, only to turn and worship a golden cow? How could they have walked through the very waters God had held back, yet grumble against him? Our minds can be quick to forget and doubt what we have seen, even if it has been awesome.

On my worst days, I look back over the events of the past twelve months and wonder, "Did that really happen?" There are some days when I don't even feel like I had a baby, although the tears and grief that are my constant companion tell me otherwise.

The journey God has taken me on throughout the course of my son's life and beyond has been truly awesome, and it is not something I want to forget. To begin with, this was the purpose of writing down my story. I didn't want to forget my son. I didn't want to forget the pain or the joy or how God has done a work in me throughout this time. In all honesty, some of the chapters of this book were written when I was suffering in some of the deepest grief. Perhaps this depressing undertone will come through to you as you read. It is an honest and raw account of my journey, but I pray it will be an encouragement to you.

I began writing this book as soon as I was able to mentally cope with facing the story in my life. However, as I have attempted to record the events of the journey, I realise that my memory is already failing me. Perhaps too much time has passed. Perhaps the grief has blinded me to some things. I have tried to write this testimony so it is a true account of the events that have occurred.

In my record of conversations, I have tried to avoid quoting people directly unless I distinctly remember the words they used. When I have quoted people, perhaps the words are not exactly correct, but they are true representations of what I (and my husband) remember from these conversations. Of course, what we say and what someone else takes from a conversation may not always be the same thing, and I hope you will take this into consideration as you read.

As I have progressed further and further into writing this book, God continues to do a great work in me. I have already been blessed by the opportunity to share my testimony by way of speaking engagements, and I am already astounded by the feedback that comes my way. There are the usual remarks of encouragement and appreciation for my speaking (which are deeply appreciated), but the comment that keeps reoccurring is, "You're so honest!"—as though it is something unusual.

In many ways, this saddens me. Of course, it is one thing to stand before a large group of people and tell them what a filthy sinner you are and how you have failed in your own life and in your

Introduction

walk with God. Not everyone is going to be game enough to do that. But as more and more feedback comes my way, I am increasingly concerned about the lack of honesty that seems to be shown in private Bible study groups or even in godly relationships. One lady even told me that in the Bible study she attends, whenever a particularly personal question comes up, the leader suggests that they do that question at home in their own time so as not to make anyone uncomfortable.

What a shame it is that we have become this way. In the corporate sense, it is so hypocritical of us to put on shiny, happy Christian faces, blindly claiming the promise that God will work all things for good in our lives (Rom. 8:28) yet inwardly being angry with him and at worst, doubting that he is even there. Even more concerning to me, though, is if this is the corporate facade, what is the facade in our own private relationship with God? How can we ever allow God to do a work in us if we are not brutally honest with ourselves and the state we are in because of our own sin? How can we repent if we do not first recognise our sin?

When I have told people bits and pieces about my journey, again and again people tell me I am being too hard on myself. On the whole, this comment bothers me greatly. It is true in some sense; I have learned there are times when I am too hard on myself. I expected my grief to be intense but ultimately short and that I would be able to move on with my life. Not so. I expected that I would not suffer in my faith or my relationship with God because I had trusted him in every way. Not so. This remark about being too hard on oneself is perhaps usefully limited to these few aspects.

Generally what I find when we say we are too hard on ourselves is that we don't want to come to terms with our own sin. If we feel guilty about the way we parent or the way we interact with another person, the guilt is usually there for a reason. We have done something poorly. We have even sinned. Telling ourselves that we are simply being too hard on ourselves is an easy way for us to excuse our sin.

I am not suggesting that God's grace isn't big enough for us. It is bigger than we can imagine. What I am saying is that we need to acknowledge sin for what it is, and it is not pretty. In fact, it is so horrendous that God himself died to get rid of it. It is an abomination.

What started out as a selfish endeavour to faithfully recount the events of my son's life for the sake of my other children and the family and friends who have walked through this journey with us has also turned into something else. This book is about sin—my sin and the sin that is in the world. This is because without the sin, we fail to see the magnitude of the grace.

More than anything, I want this book to encourage you. I want to encourage you to be as honest with both Christians and non-Christians as I am with you in this book. Don't sugar-coat the gospel. It doesn't need it. God's love is the sweetest thing we will ever know. God's love endures whatever we can throw at it: our sin, our faithlessness, or our anger. Just read the Bible. It is full of sinful men and women who spit in God's face, yet his love endures. The moment we try to gloss up the gospel to make it look more attractive to other people, we actually insult him. It's as if we are standing up and saying that God's grace is the cherry on top, but our faith and works are the substance. In actual fact, the only reason we are standing at all is by God's grace.

At one point, I was so worried that I would never be able to publish this story—that my faith would fall completely to pieces and God wouldn't come through. If it had been left up to me and my so-called faith, this is what would have happened. It would have been a file on my computer I would have left behind for my children to one day read about their brother. But that is the magnificence and awesomeness of God's grace and faithfulness. He does come through, even when we have lost all hope. In fact, he

Introduction

himself says that it is in our weakness that his power is made perfect (2 Cor. 12:9). This is a very difficult idea to get our heads around, especially if we have never been in a position where our future and the future of those most precious to us is completely and utterly at the mercy of God. Of course, it always is, but we so rarely choose to acknowledge it.

Therefore, encourage each other. Be honest with one another. If you are struggling with your faith or if you are angry with God, admit it to one another. God is so good. How can you encourage your friends, Christian or not, if you don't first admit how hopeless you are? Perhaps that is one of the reasons we are so often ineffectual in telling others how great God is. In a country like ours where most of us go without nothing (such as clean water, food, basic medical care, education, etc.) and a high proportion of us have luxuries and comforts of living that are unheard of in other parts of the world, what could a God like ours have to offer anyone? We already have the house, the car, the health insurance, the hobbies, the toys, the career, and the kids. We don't need God. What could he possibly offer us?

The sad fact is that even as Christians, we are often blessed with these things also, and we can treat God like the icing on the cake. We attribute our wealth and prosperity to him, but when something goes wrong, we can be just as lost as nonbelievers. He has to take us on a journey that shows us the true poverty of our spirits so we may rejoice in our Creator and even perhaps for the first time really see what Christ has saved us from. He has to remind us that our security is not in our health, our wealth, or even our relationships. All of these things are unstable and therefore are unreliable as a foundation for our lives. Christ alone is the only solid foundation, and as the well-known hymn aptly observes, "All other ground is sinking sand."[ii]

I leave you with these questions to consider: How can you ever really reflect the glory of Christ in your life if you, first, never come to terms with the brutality of your own sin and second, never share it with anyone? How can anyone else see his or her own desperate need for the redeeming and regenerating work of Jesus if that work is never displayed? Blessed are the poor in spirit indeed!

1

'Tis the Season to Be Jolly

"That cheesecake belongs in the fridge," I chided my mother-in-law rather curtly. It was a hot Christmas Day, and my prized Bailey's marble cheesecake was melting before my eyes. I was unimpressed, to say the least. I mean, everyone knows cheesecake belongs in the fridge, especially on hot days. Why didn't she understand that it was important to look after the dessert that had taken me a full hour to prepare? Why didn't she understand that it was disrespectful to treat my sweet offerings with such indifference? Why didn't she understand that I was in emotional hell because I was about to miscarry yet another baby—or so I thought?

In retrospect, although it was annoying that my mother-in-law had left my cheesecake unattended, my fear of losing another precious baby was what made the Christmas of 2010 a real downer. We were already blessed with two beautiful children—Allison (three years old) and Harry (two years old)—but these blessings had not come without their share of sorrow. Only two months earlier, we had miscarried at the ten-week mark—our second miscarriage out of four pregnancies in as many years.

I was only six weeks pregnant, and we were still rejoicing in the secret knowledge of our good news. Other than Michael, I had told only one good and trusted friend who I knew was praying for me about the pregnancy. But on this Christmas morning, I had felt a change. I had awoken feeling different from the past few days.

Previous experience told me that I was feeling a change in the hormone levels in my body because my baby had died. I had no other evidence of miscarriage—just a gut feeling. So I waited.

I endured the family Christmas, trying to enjoy conversation and festivities with my husband's family. It was difficult. My sister-in-law was sitting across the room sporting a beautiful baby bump. It was all I could think about. Why was this happening again?

Most women I know have suffered at least one miscarriage, and I am not exaggerating when I say most. The current statistics suggest that one in four Australian women will experience miscarriage, and miscarriage accounts for up to 30 per cent of all pregnancies.[iii] That is almost one in three pregnancies. Just pause for a moment and let those numbers sink in.

Miscarriage is an utter tragedy and not to be taken lightly. It is a deeply upsetting event, and why wouldn't it be? A life has been lost. That tiny and precious life that was just beginning is no longer.

I must admit that my grief over my miscarriages at that time was purely selfish. I have always believed that life begins at the moment of conception, but I managed to conveniently overshadow that truth with my own selfish feelings. *I* had lost the babies that *I* wanted. *I* was the one who was so hard done by. All of *my* plans were not working out. Poor *me*.

This is something the Lord has recently had to discipline me over, and it has led me down a path of both repentance and grief for my unborn babies, even years after my miscarriages. I am so ashamed to think that my grief was purely about myself and not really about the loss of my children. How blessed I am that God has shown me grace! He has not only forgiven me, but he has also allowed me to grieve. He has also really let me see for the first time that even those little souls, who physically were no more than the size of my fingernail here on earth, are thriving children in heaven being raised in his precious care. It has been a truly remarkable journey.

Over the years, I have heard a lot of responses to reports of miscarriage—both to mine and to those of friends. Some well-meaning but careless people try to provide reassurance by saying, "Don't worry, it happens all the time." These kinds of comments are unhelpful. That is like saying to a person, "People die from cancer all the time. It's just your turn, so suck it up." That's absurd. Just ask anyone who has lost a loved one to cancer. Would you dare say to him or her, "Suck it up"? It's devastating. A life is lost. Grief and suffering begin and can last for a lifetime. To act like people's losses are just "their turn" is an insult to the victims and everyone who loves them.

Some argue that miscarriage is no big deal. It's just a few cells, they say. It's not a real baby, and the emotional upset a miscarriage causes is only because of the change in hormones. To those who take this line of thought, I ask this question: if life does not begin when that first cell divides, when does it begin?

I had not told Michael, my husband, about my concerns of miscarriage when we left for his parents' house that morning. I did not want to put a damper on his Christmas Day. By the time we were travelling home that afternoon, however, he knew something was up. I had to explain myself. Through a stream of tears, I told him of the change I had felt and about my concern that another life would be lost. Silence ensued. There was nothing more to say.

It was one of the longest weeks of my life. There was still no evidence of miscarriage, yet I needed to wait until week seven for the radiographer to confirm the presence of a heartbeat. Fancy that—a heartbeat at only seven weeks.

That week was certainly a week of concentrated prayer. We fervently prayed all week, "God, please keep our baby safe. Don't let him be miscarried. Keep him safe and well, and help him to grow."

My dad drove me to the appointment. I had no one to look after my kids for me that morning, so they had to tag along. There was no way I could manage a two-year-old and a three-year-old during an ultrasound, so Dad was on deck for crowd control. He didn't say much during the trip to the doctor's office. He had driven me to multiple emergency doctors' appointments only months earlier following a miscarriage. He is an unassuming man, but he is not stupid. In spite of the fact that I didn't reveal to him the reason for the appointment, I'm sure he knew why I had to go. But my dad knows me well. He knows I don't like to give too much information away until there is something concrete to tell others about. He faithfully drove me to my appointment and waited outside during my mystery consultation.

I cannot describe the sense of relief that washed over me when I saw my little jellybean on the screen. It was a jellybean complete with a heartbeat and all within normal measurements for a seven-week foetus. Praise God! What a blessing! I couldn't wait to get home and call Michael to tell him the good news. All was well. Our prayer was answered. God had kept our baby safe!

Most mums know that the first twelve weeks of pregnancy are the highest risk. We were seven weeks down and had five to go. Registering a heartbeat was the first hurdle we had to cross, and it was a promising sign. Given our history of miscarriage, we were guarded about sharing the news too early, so we decided wait until twelve weeks. In the meantime, our earnest prayers continued. "God, please keep our baby safe. Don't let him be miscarried. Keep him safe and well, and help him to grow."

As the weeks went by, my fatigue and nausea increased, which was a good sign. My previous pregnancies had always left me feeling nauseated until around twenty weeks, accompanied by low blood pressure and excessive fatigue. This pregnancy was certainly ticking all the boxes. Running around after a pre-schooler and a toddler only exacerbated these symptoms, and it was not long before I was saying to Michael, "This is it. *No more kids* after this baby. I cannot do this ever again."

Yes, things were ticking along nicely. I was watching my belly stretch bit by bit, even if no one else really noticed. You see, my figure has always leaned towards what might be described as voluptuous. Doctors tend to have a less-flattering term for my body shape, but I like the sound of voluptuous better. Consequently, it was not difficult to hide my small baby bump. It was still just our little secret for now.

My husband, bless him, did what he could to help me and stayed out of my way—all at the same time. Fatigue plus nausea plus two pre-schoolers equals a short fuse in anyone's language. What made it worse was every time I sensed Michael avoiding asking me questions or entering into discussions because he knew the truth would upset me, it only made me more irate. All I wanted was a good argument and to be right. I *was* right, darn it! And he just didn't *understand*. Hormones had nothing to do it. I was being perfectly rational. Why he was cowering in a corner gently rocking back and forth was beyond me.

Well, not quite. However, there is something to be gleaned from the pregnancy experience for husbands and other family members alike. It is true that pregnant women may experience, ahem ... let's say, fluctuating mood swings and intense emotions. What needs to be understood, however, is that there is often a good reason why pregnant women react in such a way. Just because we might fly off the handle when wet towels are left on the bed does not mean that our expectation of wet towels *not* being left on the bed is unreasonable. Just because we end up in a pool of tears because a random shopper comments on our poor mothering ability if we happen to forget to bring a beanie for our child on an unseasonably cold day does *not* mean that the comment from the random shopper wasn't inappropriate. These, of course, are purely hypothetical situations.

I hasten to add that raging hormones or not, us women are still required to exercise self-control. It is, after all, a fruit of the spirit. However, you could ask many women who suffer from PMS, and they will tell you that whatever tree the fruit of the spirit grows on seems to be seasonal—perhaps a monthly season. Nevertheless, self-control is our goal.

However, there are just some days when you walk into your kids' bedroom to find cornflakes, chocolate spread, and honey plastered on the bed sheets. On those occasions, you are going to be inclined to respond with an outburst. This is another totally hypothetical situation, of course. We must keep in mind that just because this reaction might be instinctive does not mean it is always justified. God tells us we are to be slow to anger and abounding in love.[iv] When you look at these trials of parenthood compared against the patience God, it continually shows us as we repeatedly sin against him. It provides greater motivation for us to control our anger and frustration.

So what is the lesson here? The lesson is that you have a choice. As a Christian and as a human, you have been given free will, and you can choose how you will respond in any situation, even though emotions may make the godly response incredibly difficult on occasion.

Our summons to the doctor's office only hours after our twenty-week scan was one such occasion. What were we to think when only two or so hours after our ultrasound scan, we were both summonsed to see the specialist at the hospital the following day? This didn't sound good. The nurse who called us gave us no further information, and the lack of information was what concerned us. Immediately it was difficult to think of anything else. It was three o'clock in the afternoon, and our appointment was at eleven o'clock the following morning. We had twenty whole hours to wait.

As I look back, I can now see how the decision we made in those few painful hours to trust God set the tone for the rest of our journey ahead. Were we concerned? Yes! Rest and sleep did not come easily that night. We kept discussing various scenarios, and we always came to the conclusion "Well, perhaps there is a complication, but I'm sure they will be able to do some surgery to fix the problem." But no matter how much we discussed our fears and tried to reassure ourselves, there was still a great and total unknown. How were we going to choose to respond to this?

Even from the start of this journey, God had his hand upon us. He gave us the faith and grace to trust him. Even in those hours when we had unsettled, troubled minds, God's peace was under it all. We had trusted God with the lives of our other children and had already been praying for this little one. God had been faithful and answered our prayers, and we knew beyond a shadow of a doubt that God was in control. We chose to trust him.

Going to the doctor's appointment was the first test of our faith. Ironically, Michael had taken the previous day off from work to attend the ultrasound scan with me. He had missed the scans of our first two children, and since I was convinced that this would absolutely be our last baby I suggested that he take the day off and come to see his little baby on the screen. Now, because of the mystery call from the doctor, Michael had to take a second day off work. As it happened, I had no babysitters available for the doctor's appointment, so even though we knew full well that the doctor probably had bad news, we were unable to go the appointment together. Michael stayed at home with our children, and I had to brave the obstetrician on my own.

It was a surreal feeling to sit in the waiting room in which I had waited many times before, in the same hospital where my two other children had been born. I was almost jumping out of my skin. It felt as if the second hand on the clock had slowed, and each passing second seemed like an eternity. Finally, it was time. The door swung open, and my name was called. Walking into the doctor's office was terrifying. Everything inside me twisted.

The doctor's first observation was that my husband was not with me. When I explained about our babysitting situation, he told me that it was unfortunate because he usually liked to have the husbands/partners present in these sorts of situations. This was not a good sign.

Then it came. "Mrs Boland, we have detected a problem with your baby's scan. There seems to be a problem with his brain, which I believe to be…"

Hold the phone. What?

I must admit, I did not catch the name of the condition when the doctor first said it. To make matters worse, it was not a condition the doctor was familiar with either. This was apparent because of the lack of information he was able to provide.

In fact, after his initial statement, rather than explaining to me the nature of my son's condition, the doctor thrust a printed piece of paper across the desk before me. It was one of those information sheets doctors love so much. He just pointed to it and expected me to read it while he waited.

I looked down, my mind reeling. I read the opening summary, but I don't think I took any of it in. My eyes were reading the words, but they were somehow getting lost between my eyes and my brain. How could I be expected to read a piece of paper and understand what it meant at a time like this? With a questioning look, I faced the doctor. I didn't know what to say. I didn't know what to ask.

Seeing my struggle, the doctor began to explain my son's condition in layman's terms. I think I only caught every second word. He said something about how most of his brain had not developed, and it was not a condition that could be cured. It was highly unlikely that he would be born alive, and if he was, he would not survive very long. I think that was all I really absorbed from the discussion.

Yes, that was all I absorbed from my conversation with the doctor until this definitive statement: "Mrs Boland, most people in this situation would terminate the pregnancy. That is what I would do. I have made an appointment for you at [the larger hospital in town] early this afternoon. They are waiting for you. They are a specialist feto-maternal unit and will perform another scan to more closely examine the baby's condition. They will discuss your options from there."

That was it. Appointment over. I held it together until I stepped foot out of the hospital building. To this day, I am not sure how I navigated my way back to my car through the pool of tears. How could this be happening? This is every parent's worst nightmare, and it was happening to us.

I remember calling Michael and telling him to get the kids ready to drop off at my sister's house. We needed to get to that appointment, and we were already running late. I told him I didn't want to explain things over the phone, and I didn't offer him any comfort. How could I? It was too awful. He had to wait.

Michael faithfully had the kids ready to go by the time I arrived home. We buckled them into the backseat and headed off for the first of many trips to the hospital.

The fifty-minute car ride to my sister's house was painfully slow. Michael asked me to explain what was going on, but I didn't want to discuss it in front of the kids. Simultaneously, our minds were reeling. Mine was reeling at the reality we were being faced with while his was reeling with a series of unknowns. What was going on? Why didn't I want to talk about it in front of the kids? What was so urgent that we had to drop everything and head to the hospital immediately?

We had a hard few moments dropping the kids at my sister's. We were trying to remain calm so we would not panic our kids, my sister's family, or my parents, who happened to be visiting at the time. When we explained to our family that we needed to go into the hospital for some further tests, it of course set off alarm bells. However, I am ever grateful to my family for respecting our need to get on with it without answering a million questions. We left again shortly afterwards, and I was faced with the heartbreaking task of explaining to Michael that his son was going to die.

There were not many words spoken. I repeated the very few bits of information I had retained from the doctor's visit, and then there was silence. Tears streamed down Michael's face as he digested the news in stunned silence. In honesty, I can't remember what we spoke about for the rest of the drive to the hospital. I remember feeling eager to get in to see the specialist and ask the masses of questions that were whirring around in my mind. I remember feeling utterly helpless because I understood that this type of deformity was not one that could be corrected by surgery. I remember feeling shock and grief, but I also remember that I was not despairing. Once again, God's peace was present.

We were not kept waiting long at the hospital, and it was not many minutes before I was heaving my pregnant frame up onto the examination table, surrounded by a team of experts and specialists. I was so devastated, so broken that I couldn't even look at my baby on the screen as the technician moved the monitor over my belly. This baby—the very same baby I had enjoyed seeing for the first time only yesterday—I could not even bear to look at now. I asked the radiographer to turn the viewing monitor off, and I just listened to them as they described to Michael what they were observing.

It was not good. The diagnosis was confirmed, and for the first time, three little letters stuck in my brain: HPE. It was many weeks before I could get my mouth around the full term for the condition: holoprosencephaly. But for now, it was HPE—the bad one. There are four categories of HPE, varying from a slight malformation of the brain that can have little bearing on a person's overall functionality and quality of life, to the most severe form (Alobar), which means that baby may not even be born alive, and even if he is, he will have a very short life expectancy and will never progress beyond the ability level of a newborn. Alobar HPE was my baby's diagnosis.

I listened as the doctor explained to my husband that HPE is a condition where the brain fails to divide properly or at all into the two spheres. All of the stem and base of the baby's brain appeared to be developing normally, but the space in the head where the grey matter of the brain should have been present was mostly a dark cavity of fluid, with a small, crescent-shaped portion of grey matter to one side.

The implications of his condition were largely unknown. Again and again the doctors reinforced that our baby would not survive, and even if he did, we had no way of knowing how the wiring of the brain that was present would affect him. Even if the rest of his body had developed normally (which was also an unknown at that stage), his brain might not be able to signal to his body so his organs could function normally. It was a great, great unknown.

We had many questions and put them to the specialist in charge. I am unsure of whether the doctor was being deliberately evasive in his responses, but we didn't seem to be getting any solid answers. We wanted to know what the likelihood was that I would be able to carry the baby to full term. We wanted to know if there was a chance he would live, even in a severely debilitated state. We wanted to know how we could help our baby.

Perhaps the following remark is unfair to the practitioners and staff members who were present, but I remember walking away with this clear message from the doctors: You should terminate. There is no hope. You can gather all of the information you like, but most people can't go through with the pregnancy because it's too difficult. There is no hope for your baby. There is no value to his life.

I know in the appointment that the doctors and staff were attempting to sound very liberal in their approach. They said things like, "There is no right or wrong decision here" or "Don't make any decision just now." However, everything else they suggested and every other action they took reinforced that termination was the most sensible and practical answer. Even after we told them that termination was not a path we were prepared to go down, they repeated these answers.

Since we had not had many of our questions answered and we really did not have a great understanding of our baby's condition, we requested to see a geneticist at the suggestion of the specialist. We were not sure what a geneticist was or how he would be able to help, but we needed some answers. We were promptly given an appointment for the following day. This was a relief for us because we did not want to wait over the weekend to ask our questions.

Our journey home from the hospital was filled with discussion. We made a list of the questions we already had. We talked about the unhelpfulness of the specialist at the hospital. We held hands and cried together.

We were one in our questions, one in our grief. Without any prior discussion, we also found that we were one on another front. Our baby was a gift from the Lord. We would not be terminating this pregnancy.

2
What's in a Name?

I'm not sure what reaction I expected my mother-in-law to have. We decided to detour past her house on our way home and break the news to her in person. As with most things, it was a good thing that we did not have an expectation of what people's reactions would be. If I had, perhaps I might have thought she would cry with us. She didn't. She just sat there in shock, not knowing what to say. What was there to say? She did not have many questions because she could see we were in a state of shock ourselves. There were so many unknowns. It was a short visit, and we left her to share the news with Da.

We arrived home not long before my parents arrived home with our children. I am sure they sensed my reluctance to explain the outcome of our appointment in front of the kids, so we spent a surreal afternoon of small talk and routine. Mum and Dad live in a self-contained flat attached to our house, and as I had done many times since they moved in with us, I appreciated their presence and assistance with our children.

We put the children to bed, and the moment had come to tell my parents about our baby's condition. We went through it all again and watched as they sat in stunned silence. There were no tears on their part and plenty on ours.

As we were explaining the situation, I remember thinking to myself that if this baby was not going to survive until full term (which was a distinct possibility from what we had been told), I hoped I would miscarry the baby sooner rather than later. When Mum and Dad asked how they could pray for us in this situation, I asked that the Lord would take him soon. It was a selfish prayer and one I am so glad in hindsight that God didn't answer with yes.

This was a selfish prayer because I was not praying it to spare my baby pain and hardship, even though that is what I thought I was doing at the time. I wanted to save myself the pain. This pregnancy had already been filled with trials of sickness and fatigue, and I felt I couldn't face the pain of a full-term stillborn baby on top of it all. We were not going to make any moves to deliberately terminate the pregnancy, but I prayed, "Lord, if you take him, it's okay with us. *Please* take him. Spare *us* the hardship." Selfish, selfish, selfish.

This was the first of many times throughout our journey when I was surprised by just how selfish our sinful nature is. It might come as a shock to many people that my initial reaction to our baby's condition was, "How will this affect me?" not "Oh, my poor baby!" Yet there it was. I was devastated. I was devastated for myself. I was devastated for my husband. Everything we had wanted for our family, for ourselves, was in jeopardy. Oh yes, and poor baby.

In general terms, if those of us who are parents look at how we actually parent and are brutally honest with ourselves, we must be forced to admit how selfish we can be. Children are supposed to bring out the best in us, right? We are supposed to give unconditional love, selfless sacrifice, and all the rest. Yet our approach to parenting is often extremely selfish. Oh yes, we can bury it under a lot of other things and label it as love, but at the heart of the matter, it is selfish behaviour.

We fail to discipline our kids because *we* feel badly doing it. It makes *us* feel bad to make our kids feel bad, so we don't, and our kids suffer with upbringings where no boundaries are set and they

What's in a Name?

are not required to respect parental authority (or any authority, for that matter). On the occasions when we do discipline our kids, it is often because they displayed annoying behaviour. It is because they have done something to annoy us or to embarrass us.

They have broken the vase. They have thrown their food on the floor. They have had a tantrum at the shops. These are all terribly inconvenient, costly, and quite annoying. We move to correct their behaviour not because we want to teach them a correct way to behave so they might be thoughtful and respectful contributors to society and obedient to God. Instead it is so we don't have to put up with annoying or embarrassing behaviour. Oh yes, parenting has the potential to be very selfish indeed. We can love our kids deeply, but we can still parent selfishly. It has a hard truth, and one I was faced with.

At this point I must say that in the majority of cases, the termination of a pregnancy falls into this same category. It is so easy to have an unborn baby diagnosed with an illness or condition and convince ourselves that it is better for the child if he or she were not to be born. However, if we were honest about our motivations, it is because it's easier for *us* not to have to raise a child with an illness or a condition. There are complications and expenses. Fulltime care may be needed. Equipment and medication will be required. Parents who are enjoying the benefits of a successful career may have to give up work to care for their child—perhaps for the rest of their lives. Parents who already have children may have to devote themselves more to one child than another in practical terms. That is a lot of sacrifice.

Even in the case of unwanted or accidental pregnancy, the decision to terminate is almost always made because of the strain and disruption that would be put on the lives that are already out of the womb. A teenage girl falls pregnant, yet having the baby will mean many years of struggle, a postponed or halted education, scorn, ridicule, financial struggles, loss of freedom—the list goes on. Some of these situations (and some more than others) are very real and extremely tough, and many of these factors must be seriously considered and worked through. However, the ugly fact remains that these reasons in themselves as motivation for termination are ultimately selfish.

Our trip to the geneticist was informative. She told us some of the ins and outs of the HPE condition and that it was estimated that 1 in every 250 pregnancies has a baby suffering from HPE. However, out of those 1 in 250 pregnancies, it is estimated that only 1 in 5,000 babies suffering with HPE will make it past twelve weeks of gestational age, with the other pregnancies ending in miscarriage.[v] Now I am no math whiz, but by my calculations, this already put our baby at 1 in 1,250,000 odds. The fact that he had survived to twenty-one weeks was astounding in itself.

All through the meeting with the genetic counsellors, we sensed a lack of understanding on their part as to why we would not terminate the pregnancy. As I mentioned earlier, they were very liberal in their approach when they talked about our options, citing time and time again that there was no right or wrong course of action—only whatever was best for us.

They even went as far as to say that if we decided to terminate our pregnancy, no one need know about it. Yes, that's right—we were actually encouraged in our appointment to not only terminate our unborn baby's life but also to lie to our family and friends about it. Obviously people were going to recognise that I was no longer pregnant, but our doctors suggested, "No one needs to know why." Could it be that they were actually suggesting we terminate our pregnancy and pass it off as a miscarriage to avoid judgment from our family and friends?

I would like to take a moment just to process this with you. Think about this very carefully. In this country, there has been an increasing push for the awareness of mental illnesses, such as depression and anxiety. We even have an annual national "Are You

What's in a Name?

Okay? Day" where work colleagues and acquaintances are encouraged to ask each other, "Are you really okay?"

Let me be clear: I support the idea of looking out for the wellbeing of those we come into contact with. However, isn't it sad that our relationships are so superficial that we have to institute a day to ask the question? So many are suffering silently because they are not being honest with the people in their lives about the struggles they are facing and the emotions they are experiencing.

Here we were facing some of the most devastating news a parent could hear, and we were actually being encouraged to kill our child and not tell anyone about it. Fancy being responsible for ending your own child's life and then not being able to deal with the emotional fallout with anyone close to you. Fancy being responsible for the death of your children's baby brother/sister, your parents' grandchild, your sister's nephew/niece, and them never knowing. This is not the stuff of close, healthy relationships. A secret like this will fester away at your mind and your relationships and may very well lead you down a path of mental illness. Furthermore, it will create a distance in your otherwise close relationships and will leave you with no one to walk that path with you.

Surely this logic alone should ring alarm bells that something is not right with the option of termination. Let's put aside for a moment (if we can) the issue of killing your own child. What about the issue of lying to your family and friends? Any lie in a relationship only creates distance, even those lies which are meant for good.

What would you think of a husband who lied to his wife over the course of thirty years of marriage, pandering to her ego and telling her she was a kind and good daughter to her parents even though he really knows she treats her parents like rubbish? Does it do her any favours in the long run? No! Not only would there be distance between the couple because he knows something she does not, but she also would not able to correct her behaviour towards her parents because it would have been reinforced to her as good and proper behaviour, thus creating distance between her and her parents also. Lies always create distance in relationships, and their effects can be more far-reaching and devastating than we can fathom.

Perhaps it would be prudent to discuss the other side of facing the judgment of friends and family. Judgment always stems from a matter of opinion. We all judge others based on our opinion of a situation or in line with our life philosophies (for want of a better word). As Christians, there will often be times when we must act in ways that will go against the grain of society, and we will be persecuted for it. Peter tells us it will be inevitable yet glorious to be persecuted for the sake of Christ because it means that we are doing something right (see 1 Peter 4:12–19).

There are many people and causes in the world who are not afraid to stand up for what they believe in, both Christians and non-Christians. Let me tell you that the ones who are honest about their lives and beliefs are the ones who sleep well at night. To be clear, I am not saying that all causes that are upheld by those who are openly and honestly fighting for them are worthwhile causes. Many of them are not. What I am saying is that if we are not honest about who we are, what we are doing, or why we are doing what we are doing, we are living false lives, and living a false life will eventually tear you apart. Secular society calls this "being true to yourself." As a Christian, this is called facing the facts. In either context, it is a testimony to God's Word.

God's Word is all about truth. It is the *only* truth. The funny thing about truth is that there is only one truth. Anything else is a lie. Nevertheless, we live in a postmodern society where truth is synonymous with point of view. We are led to believe that there are many truths. We are very liberal in saying, "Well, that works for him, and this works for me" without any deeper thought as to how

What's in a Name?

dangerous that actually is. The belief that perspective is truth is a dangerous thing.

Imagine I had a cup of sand. Let's say someone came over to my house and insisted that the cup of sand was actually a cup of salt. He *genuinely* believed it was a cup of salt. Perhaps I could understand why he believed it was a cup of salt. Salt looks a bit like sand, it's sort of the same weight as sand, and it feels the same as sand. He could try cooking with it like he would cook with salt. At a glance, no one would be able to tell it was really sand, but at the first mouthful, the difference would be evident. His belief that the sand was actually salt did not change the reality. The notion in itself is ludicrous. It was sand all along.

In some sense, the same could be said of God. Whether a person chooses to believe in God or what he or she believes about God does not actually change the fact that God exists or who he is. The notion is similarly ludicrous. We can come up with all sorts of things in our lives that imitate God, but when you learn who God really is, all of that false stuff is like taking a mouthful of sand. It is easy to see the difference. The deceptions can only get us so far.

In fact, they can get us very far. Think of the millions of souls who have passed on thinking they have lived full lives because they have had money, health, and children who love them. To be sure, there is a level of joy and satisfaction to be had from all of these things, but in themselves, they are meaningless. To say that someone who has had all of these things has lived a more valuable or happy life than someone who has been poor, suffered ill-health, and never had children is simply a matter of opinion. If you take God out of the equation, the measure of a good life is purely a matter of opinion. This seems to me to be very shaky ground for the thousands out there who are genuinely trying to live a good life without God.

Furthermore, consider what is at stake. God is who he says he is. Therefore, the truth is that those who die who do not know

Jesus will spend eternity removed from God suffering torment beyond our comprehension. It makes no difference whether they believe this will happen.

For nonbelievers, that is a very big risk to take, even from a purely logical perspective. What if they are wrong? They often exercise caution with their finances by not gambling their wealth, but they are prepared to gamble their eternal future on their own belief about the odds, as if what they believe actually changes the reality of the situation. And this is precisely my point. It makes no sense at all, yet so many of the big questions of life are simply too hard for us to think about or come to terms with the consequences, so we tend to believe the lie because it makes us more comfortable. It is short-sighted, self-serving, and totally illogical.

The truth is that terminating a pregnancy is ending your child's life. It does not matter what perspective you take; that is the truth of the situation. You can add perspective to that fact, but the fact does not change. And it's adding the ungodly perspectives (i.e., the views that are not founded in truth) that cause us to be undone. The government's laws about life in utero are a perfect example. As John Piper so accurately surmises, "If she wants her baby, it's illegal to kill it (foetal homicide). If she doesn't, it's not (abortion)."[vi]

The geneticist explained to us that the cause of HPE in our baby might be genetic or it might just be an "accident of nature." But being the clever human beings we are, it is possible to run a genetic analysis of the amniotic fluid to see whether the deformation was genetically caused. This is a procedure called an amniocentesis, and it is performed by inserting a needle into mum's pregnant belly (with the guide of an ultrasound) and extracting a small amount of fluid from within the placenta.

It was at this moment that Michael and I were presented with our first decision. Should we proceed with an amniocentesis? The results of the test would not help our baby, but they might

What's in a Name?

provide genetic information that would identify a gene in our family line that might cause HPE. The geneticist explained that this could assist us with future family planning or family planning for our children.

From what we understood from the information provided, the genetic information from the amniotic fluid would not be available to the geneticists unless they were to perform an autopsy on our son (a procedure I just could not bear to think about). Statistically, there is a 1 in 200 chance of miscarriage after an amniocentesis is performed.[vii] What should we do?

It had only been a matter of days since we had learned of our baby's complications. We were in shock, and our heads were still swimming from the volume of information that was sent our way. The geneticist was putting pressure on us to make a decision quickly because I was already at twenty-two weeks and they do not like to perform an amniocentesis after twenty-three weeks.

In hindsight, the amniocentesis for us was a moot point. At the time, after discussion and prayer, Michael and I decided to proceed with it on the grounds that it could help us with potential future pregnancies and for our other children's pregnancies if the condition was found to be genetic. However, we made this decision without recognising what the "family planning" referred to by the geneticist actually involved. This type of family planning involves testing embryos or amniotic fluid in future pregnancies for early detection of the condition and the subsequent disposal (aka abortion) of embryos or foetuses carrying the deformity. This was a process we would never consent to be a part of.

Nevertheless, we went ahead with the procedure, entrusting the care of our son to the Lord. It was the first time in the few days that had passed where I found myself praying that the Lord would keep him safe. It was in many ways a naive prayer, but it was genuine all the same. I can now see the grace that God showed to us in so many ways in this situation. First, he had already begun to change my heart. A few days earlier, I had been more than willing to receive prayer that I would miscarry and have it over and done with quickly. Now here I was praying that my son would be kept safe from this procedure. Not only that, but I realise now how hypocritical we were to put our child at a 1 in 200 risk for absolutely no reason. There was no possible outcome of this genetic testing that would make one ounce of difference in our lives or in the life of our baby. What an unnecessary risk. Yet God showed us more grace and kept us both safe.

On the drive home after the procedure, a conversation I had with Michael showed me that God had changed his heart too. Only days before, we were frightened and anxious about what the future held, but as we talked, we realised that for the first time since hearing the news, we were both looking forward to meeting our little boy more than ever.

Our discussion soon turned to how to break the news to our other children. Up until this point, our kids had been out of the loop. At the time, Allison was three and Harry was two. This was a difficult situation to explain to our children, who were already so excited about the baby growing in Mummy's tummy. We knew they would be heartbroken, even if they didn't fully understand. We wanted them to know that things were not right. We didn't want to lie to them and pretend everything was well. This was their journey as well. What an opportunity to grow together as a family. What an opportunity to show our kids the love and grace of God.

But how should we do it? It was in the midst of these questions that we decided to make our son a big part of our family right away—far bigger than we would in other pregnancies. Our son was to be included as part of the family from that point on. We would talk about him a lot. We would tell the kids that he was very sick and the doctors would not be able to make him better. We would get a nursery ready for him, and the kids would be involved in getting ready for a new member of the family.

What's in a Name?

Some people are inclined to be critical of this decision. We are often tempted to protect our children from pain and suffering, even at the expense of the truth. Of course there is a time for protecting our children and being selective with what is shared. However, this baby was not just our child; he was their brother also. How could we deny them the excitement we felt? How could we deny them the pain they would feel in losing their brother? If we were to shield our children by making it less important than it was, not only would we not have been honest, but we also would have robbed them of the opportunity to love and miss their brother and experience God's grace in their lives.

It's interesting how stories come out of the woodwork. Since having Stephen, I have been surprised to learn of so many people already in my life who have suffered similar loss. A baby brother. A baby son. A baby sister. In a culture bursting at the seams with medical information and services, we still have two thousand stillborn children every year in Australia, which is roughly 1 stillborn child to every 135 live births.[viii]

A neighbour of ours has a daughter-in-law who had a baby sibling die when she was a young girl. It was never talked about in her home. Her Mum and Dad moved on (or tried to), and as my neighbour observed, the news of our son's condition in their family brought so many deep-rooted emotions to the surface for this young woman that she was in fact grieving for her own sibling. Almost twenty years later, her grief had not been dealt with because she was not allowed to grieve in her home as a child.

This was not something we wanted for Allison and Harry. This is not something we wanted for our son. He was our son, and we were determined to treat him with the love, care, and respect we have for all of our children. We needed to make the most of every opportunity we had with our son because we didn't know how long we would have him as part of our family. Oh, how we had taken all of our pregnancies for granted! Now it was different. It had to be.

Almost at the same moment, we both blurted out, "He needs a name." We already had a short list of girls' names and boys' names chosen, but we had made no decision. As soon as the topic was raised, my husband said, "His name is Stephen."

Stephen? That name wasn't on our short list. We had never even considered it. It's not even a name I particularly liked. As it turns out, it's not even a name Michael liked either. Since finding out the news about our son, however, it seemed Michael could not get the name Stephen out of his mind. So Stephen it was. *Stephen*. Our boy had a name. How I have come to love and cherish that name. When I arrived home, I sought out my naming book to find out what the name means.

When I looked up the name, at the time I didn't really understand why God had chosen Stephen. I knew that Stephen had been the first Christian martyr in the New Testament, but that was really as far as I'd thought. Almost a year after choosing his name, I came across this description of Stephen in my Bible dictionary, and it brought a smile to my face.

> STEPHEN (Gk. stephanos, 'crown'). Stephen was one of the seven men chosen by the disciples soon after the resurrection to look after the distribution of assistance to the widows of the church, so that the apostles themselves should be freed for their spiritual tasks...Stephen is recorded as standing out from the others in faith, grace, spiritual power, and wisdom (Acts 6:5, 8, 10). He had time to do more than the special work assigned to him, for he

was among the foremost in working miracles and preaching the gospel.

He soon fell foul of the Hellenistic synagogue, which brought him before the Sanhedrin on charges of blasphemy (6:9-14). Stephen, with angelic face, replied to the charges with a survey of the history of Israel and an attack upon the Jews for continuing in the tradition of their fathers and killing the Messiah (6:15-7:53). This brought upon him the fury of the council, and when he claimed to see Jesus standing at the right hand of God (probably as his advocate or witness in his defence) he was seized and stoned to death (7:54-60). He met his end courageously, as did his Master, on accusations by false witnesses of seeking to overthrow the Temple and law (cf. Mt. 26:59-61). He prayed as Jesus had done (Lk, 23:46) for his persecutors to be forgiven and committed his soul into Christ's keeping (cf. Lk. 23:46)...

There were striking consequences from Stephen's death. The persecution which followed (Acts 8:1) led to a more widespread preaching of the gospel (8:4; 11:19). Stephen's death was also undoubtedly a factor in bringing Saul of Tarsus to Christ (7:58, 8:1, 3; 22:20). But above all, Stephen's speech was the beginning of a theological revolution in the early church, as the principles of the universal mission were clearly stated for the first time.[ix]

3

A Hart of Compassion

A look of bewilderment like I have never before seen covered his face. We were back at our local hospital, breaking the news to our obstetrician that we were not going to terminate the pregnancy. Clearly he had not expected this news. He shifted uncomfortably in his seat as he realised the impact of what we were saying and how it affected him. He was not rude, but he was far from empathetic. For a small-town doctor, this was clearly outside of his comfort zone. He had never managed a case of HPE in his career, and he didn't seem keen to start now. Since I was well enough and Stephen was otherwise as well as could be expected, the specialist hospital in town didn't want to know me. I had been referred back to my local obstetrician for prenatal care.

We tried explaining to the doctor that we valued Stephen's life as much as those of our other children, and we wanted him to receive the same level of care as any other healthy child. His life had value and was precious in our eyes and the eyes of God. Now let me just say that I did not expect every medical practitioner to share our view on the value of life in the eyes of God. However, this was the first of many times I was to be shocked, heartbroken, and ashamed to hear the value others placed on a life. When we said these things to our doctor, his response was, "Well, that all depends on how you measure the value of life." I'm sorry, did I miss something? Was my doctor suddenly God and the authority on the measure of a man's life?

It was our turn to look bewildered. Our doctor went on to explain that in medical terms, the value of life is measured by hope. His implication was that in his professional opinion, Stephen's life was not worth the hassle and the care he would require (or I dare say, not worth the taxpayer's dollar) because there was no hope for his life. He was not expected to live. The doctor even took it one step further and attempted to draw a comparison between an adult on life support and our baby. If there is no hope for a person on life support, doctors pull the plug. I want you to think very closely about that analogy for a moment. It will not take more than a moment for you to see why that analogy makes no sense at all and is in fact an insult.

It took all my self-control to not lean over the desk and punch the doctor in the mouth. I decided that not only was that a fairly ungodly approach to the situation, but it was also not the smartest move because he was the only public obstetrician close to our home. If he had a restraining order against my husband and me, it was going to make prenatal check-ups rather a challenge.

Seeing that our mind was made up, the doctor had no choice but to agree to oversee my pregnancy and care. He could see we had many questions regarding what the future might hold for a baby born with HPE, so he referred us for an urgent consultation with one of the paediatricians practicing at the hospital.

Underwhelmed by the lack of support from our doctor, we returned home. Could it really be that this was the attitude and care we would receive for the course of our pregnancy? And if this was the doctor's attitude towards us now, how would Stephen be treated once he was born? If doctors were reluctant to care for him now, what difference would it make whether he was in the womb or out?

We had about two weeks to wait until our appointment with the paediatrician. In the meantime, our questions abounded. What were the physical and practical implications for a baby born with HPE? What did it mean for us as parents? What sorts of complications were likely? How long could we expect Stephen to live for if he was born alive? We needed information, and like most children of this technological era, we turned to the Internet for answers.

It was difficult to find information about HPE. There were some nice overall definitions on various sites, but it was difficult to find anything beyond a general explanation. We eventually found a useful site that was run by Families for HoPE, Inc.,[x] which is an organisation run in America that seeks to provide support for families in all stages in the HPE journey. This site has been hugely helpful for us, and we found links to a number of medical research papers and testimonies that have helped us and encouraged us along the way.

In this information-gathering stage, our hearts began to sink as we realised the seriousness of Stephen's condition. Up to this point, we had understood that he would be severely disabled and was not going to progress beyond the capability of a newborn child, but we had not yet realised the related complications. Suddenly we were reading that many children born with Alobar HPE have trouble regulating their body temperature, causing both drops and peaks of extreme levels in body temperature that would require hospitalisation. We also learned that feeding would be a problem. Babies with Alobar HPE need to be tube fed and eventually peg fed through the belly-button (if they lived long enough). Epileptic-type seizures were also common in HPE babies.

There was also a high possibility that fluid would build up in the cavity where his brain was supposed to be and cause his head to swell. This condition would require a surgery where a shunt would be inserted into the cavity and run down into the stomach to drain excess fluid. Of course, there were countless complications with all of these matters, and it scared the socks off us to think about what our lives might look like in the coming years.

You see, one of the great difficulties with HPE is that so many of the complications are totally unforeseeable. It all depends on what the portion of brain that is present is able to control and how. For example, a baby's digestive system may work, but the kidneys may not. In such an instance, the baby could potentially be put on a form of needle dialysis if he was going to be fed. This was only one of countless potential difficulties. Did we really have the capacity to care for a child who needed such a high level of care?

When the day came for our appointment with the paediatrician, we sat in Dr Hart's waiting room. I watched him usher his patients and their parents in and out of his office. I had seen him once before when Allison was a baby, and he was one of those doctors you instantly warmed to. He was a gentle, kind, and personable man who genuinely loved his job. I had been so thrilled when the obstetrician referred us to Dr Hart. I knew we were in kind hands.

We weren't disappointed. We guessed Dr Hart had spent the time between ushering out his last patient and calling us in familiarising himself with Stephen's rare condition. As soon as we sat down opposite him, we saw our pain mirrored in his face. His first words to us were the most compassionate words said by any doctor throughout the entire course of Stephen's life. In a slow and sombre manner that was appropriate to the gravity of the situation, he began.

"I can't imagine what it is like to be put in this situation, and I see you have come to the decision to continue with the pregnancy. I am here to help you and support you in any way that I can and to do whatever I can for your baby. By the way, does he have a name yet?"

He asked for a name. *He asked for a name!* Could it be that this doctor actually acknowledged value in our little boy's life, enough to ask for a name? In retrospect, the words he spoke were not grand or even emotional. But after all the negativity we had received from medical professionals, it was like a breath of fresh air. Finally, here was someone who saw the value in our boy's life—someone who did not question the value we placed on our son's life.

We immediately felt that Dr Hart had Stephen's best interests at heart. We were able to ask him many questions and not second-guess the motives behind his answer. What a blessing Dr Hart was to us. He told us he planned to be present at the birth to make an initial assessment of Stephen's health. What we hadn't realised as Dr Hart continued was what a huge can of worms of we were opening. There were so many questions we had not considered and had no answer for. Would we resuscitate if Stephen was not born breathing but seemed to be otherwise healthy? And if so, how could we justify resuscitating him the first time and not subsequent times if he became ill?

And what if he became ill? Knowing that the overall prognosis of his life was not great, how would we decide to provide medical intervention, and when would we decide to stop? Was it right to keep using every medical avenue available to prolong his little life? How could we justify using medical technology to bring him into the world safely and then refuse that same technology to keep him alive? Was it ethical? And more importantly, was it godly?

Dr Hart did his best to answer our medical questions, but we could see that even he was struggling to provide answers. We were overwhelmed. We had known there would be complications, but we had never given consideration to these deeper issues. As we left Dr Hart, we were already praying—praying for direction. How were we to answer these questions? How were we to face what was ahead?

Since we became Christians, Michael and I have always known that all answers are found in Jesus—a fact that Jesus has proven to us time and time again. More often than not, those answers are revealed to us through his Word, the Bible, accompanied by a lot of prayer and reflection. The trouble was, in the past when we had questions or difficult situations, we had an inclining of where to begin looking for an answer. For example, for questions relating to a man's faith, the book of Hebrews is a great place to start. For questions relating to sexual sin, almost any of Paul's letters to the churches are excellent starting points.

But in a world where modern technology and medical science has changed the way we live our daily lives and has had influence over what we deem to be responsible parenting, both of us were lost as to where to start. There was nothing in the Bible, as far as we knew, about deciding when to stop trying to help your child if death was imminent. At this point we had been told that Stephen's life span was likely at best to be a few days. Even if he was a healthy boy in every other way (which every scan indicated), something as menial as a cold or a little difficulty breathing without intervention would more than likely cost him his life. Yet a small level of intervention might make the difference between him living for many more days or at a real stretch, months. Who were we to have such say?

It is all well and good to quote Psalm 139:16, which says "Your eyes saw my unformed substance; in your book were written, every one of them, the days that were formed for me, when as yet there was none of them." But how did that help us to practically make these decisions? Just because God knew ahead of time what was going to happen and what decisions we were going to make did not help us come to those decisions.

So how could we go about making such decisions? What was the godly approach in this situation? As we prayed and reflected during the coming days there were three things that kept coming to our minds.

First, we were being reminded that God only gives good gifts to his children. Consider the following verses:

> Children are a blessing and a gift from the LORD (Ps. 127:3 CEV).

> Every good gift and every perfect gift is from above, coming down from the Father of lights with whom there is no variation or shadow due to change (James 1:17).

> If you then, who are evil, know how to give good gifts to your children, how much more will your Father who is in heaven give good things to those who ask him! (Matt. 7:11).

Stephen was a gift, a blessing, and a heritage from the Lord. We had asked God to grant us another child, and here he was! In honesty, we had never asked the question, "Why us?" We had never doubted that Stephen was a gift from God, and as we were facing these difficult questions he was reminding us of this every step of the way.

Second, we were reminded that God is sovereign; there is nothing outside of his control. Consider these passages:

> Behold, I am the LORD, the God of all flesh. Is anything too hard for me? (Jer. 32:27).

> For I am the LORD; I will speak the word
> that I will speak, and it will be performed
> (Ezek. 12:25a).

> Are not two sparrows sold for a penny?
> And not one of them will fall to the
> ground apart from your Father. But even
> the hairs of your head are all numbered.
> Fear not, therefore; you are of more
> value than many sparrows (Matt. 10:29–
> 31).

There was no situation we were to face that was outside of God's control. Not only was he in control of every situation, but he was also with us every step of the way, directing not only our hearts and minds but also the minds of those around us.

The third idea that resounded in our minds was that God does not put on us more than we can handle with his help. First Corinthians 10:13 says:

> No temptation has overtaken you that is
> not common to man. God is faithful, and
> he will not let you be tempted beyond
> your ability, but with the temptation he
> will also provide the way of escape, that
> you may be able to endure it.

I'd like to pause here for just a moment and talk a little about theology, even though, as you may have figured out by now, I am no theologian. This passage is a classic example as to why I am no theologian (although I do consider theology to be important). I have heard discussions and arguments about this passage. Some people use this passage to argue that God does not put on us more than we can bear. Personally, I don't see how this argument stands up alone because I feel that quite often I have been in situations that I cannot face by myself without help from the Lord. The decisions we were facing for the welfare of our son were a classic example. However, in the translations I have read, the implication is that God does not ask us to act in situations that we cannot handle.

Now intellectually I could attempt to reason this out. I could say that our natural ability to resist temptation comes from God anyway because we are made in God's image, by God. Therefore the fact he does not put us in situations where we cannot resist temptation by our own ability is because he has already given us ability to resist. When he provides a means for us to walk away, this is his added grace in the situation.

I could also argue that he does put us under temptation we cannot bear alone because there is no good in us alone. I would say that the first verse has to be read in the context of the second, for why would he provide a way out if we could bear the temptation on our own?

In honesty, I could not tell you if either of these ideas (or neither of them) is actually how God works. I don't understand the how now, I didn't understand it then.

I am not trying to suggest that theology is not important. What I am suggesting is that God's word is for every man, regardless of intellect, and there is in fact far more mystery in the Bible and God's ways than we sometimes care to admit.

As Christians, we often feel the need to have things figured out to defend our faith. This stems from our own pride and the fear of man. We don't want to look stupid. We feel we should be able to explain God because if we can't, people will think we are nuts, uninformed, or both. Yet if we could explain everything about God, there would be little need for faith. Even the greatest theologians must admit there are things about God they don't understand, and the truly great ones even believe it. Personally, I am glad that I can't understand God. He wouldn't be very impressive if my average little brain could figure him out.

Perhaps God will reveal to me his ways on the topic of temptation in time. He has revealed things to me in the past that I could not reason out on my own. But as I read this passage back then, and as I read it now, there are two things I do understand. This passage is about grace and faith. God is gracious regardless of how he chooses to go about it, and he does not put us in situations we cannot endure. By faith, then, we can seek the Lord in all situations to guide us through and resist temptation. And it was his grace, in faith, that we clung to.

In our scenario, the temptation was to make decisions based on our own selfishness rather than seeking to honour our son and glorify God. Already I had been shown depths of my own selfishness that I had never thought possible, such as when I asked the Lord that I would miscarry. As I discussed the potential complications with Michael, I was shocked and dismayed to recognise even more of my own selfish nature. How could I be sure that further down the track, when I was tired and weary after caring for a child with such high needs, I wouldn't be tempted to refuse some treatment for him to put me out of hardship? It was that thought that scared me the most. For the first time, I was realising what a powerful role my own emotions could play and even get in the way of godly choices, even after years of faithfully obeying God's commands, which were sometimes in direct opposition to my natural feelings.

As we discussed and cried, discussed and cried, prayed, and cried some more, we were able to work out a basic birth plan for Stephen. The idea of treating our son in the same way we would treat any of our children sounds like a nice philosophy, but in practical terms, it was of little value. Was there any point to resuscitating him if he was born not breathing but otherwise healthy? Was there any point to prolonging his life? For a normal, healthy child, of course the answer is yes! But Stephen was different.

We agreed that we would not do anything intentionally to end Stephen's life. This was not a new notion for us or else the termination option may have seemed more appealing. We were not going to refuse to feed him and therefore starve him to death, as suggested by one doctor. We resolved to do everything in our power to make sure he did not suffer. We decided that if he needed some oxygen or some small help breathing once he was born, we would see that he got it. But beyond that, there were too many unknowns.

This was a terrifying time, but the Lord reminded us continually that he was in control and we needed to just trust him. So began the prayer that became our daily and sometimes hourly prayer for the months to follow: "Lord, we trust that you will not leave us in a situation we cannot handle. Please help us to make good decisions when we come to them. Amen."

4

And Now We Wait

My eyes were raw. I think I had spent the four weeks since Stephen's diagnosis wiping tears from my eyes. In my handbag, I carried a small bottle of night treatment oil designed for reducing bags under the eyes, just to relieve the stinging. I cried at breakfast time, and I cried at dinner. I cried at the shops, and I cried in church. The worst times by far were times when I was not preoccupied with changing nappies, preparing meals, or encouraging children.

Every time I was left alone with my thoughts, I cried. Trips in the car, showers, and bedtime were the worst. Quiet times with my Bible went out the window. Every time I sat alone in my chair ready to pray, all I could do was cry. Even so, I felt God's grace was big enough for me in that situation. I went for days, sometimes weeks, without reading my Bible. I just couldn't. There were days where the only prayer I could offer was, "Lord, help me through this day." The spirit was indeed willing, but the flesh was sorely grieved. I grieved for my son. I grieved for my husband. I saw the pain in my husband's face. No matter how we looked at the complications, there was one simple fact we couldn't ignore: we were going to have to bury our own son. How that thought churned in my mind, day and night. I don't think there was a night in that first month when I did not cry myself to sleep. Actually, I do not

And Now We Wait

think there were many nights in the months to follow when I did not cry.

So what does one do when waiting for the inevitable? Everything else to do with the pregnancy—both my health and Stephen's general health—were all on track. I was going for my monthly check-ups with the obstetrician, and things were progressing nicely.

To keep myself from having too many down times, I started a new project. I had remembered from my last marathon effort of a cross-stitch that cross-stitching was a long-term project. I decided it was a good way to fill in many hours at home and many hours waiting in doctors' surgeries. There is a gorgeous needlecraft shop not far from where we live, and my daughter and I trundled off to choose a project.

I scanned the walls for ages. It was a case of not knowing what I was looking for, but I would know it when I saw it. I wanted something that would remind me of Stephen in the months and years to come. I wanted something I could hang on my wall that would remind me of his precious life but nothing that was too morbid or childish. I felt that making something while he was still alive inside me would somehow connect me to him even after he was gone.

It was hard to find what I was looking for, but I eventually did. It was a design picturing a beautiful, soft teddy bear sitting on a table surrounded by toys with an enormous blue ribbon tied in a bow around his neck. Here was my Stephen Bear.

I eagerly took it home and sat down to begin my new project. I opened up the pattern, and when I saw the scale of what I had embarked on (any beginner cross-stitcher will know this feeling), I freaked out. It was far more complex than I had imagined. Yet, stitch by stitch, a bit at a time, my Stephen Bear has started to come to life. That cross-stitch has gone with me everywhere. I still faithfully chip away at it, week in and week out. I have taken it on at least two trips to Dubbo when visiting relatives and even one trip to New Zealand. It has been a means of sanity for me, and I am still delighting in seeing it come together.

So my hands were now taken care of, but my mind was still churning and my emotions very raw. I must admit that during this time, I withdrew from my relationships. I would still meet with friends, still go to playgroup, and still worship at church, but meaningful conversations were difficult for me. We had only told our immediate families and some very close friends about Stephen's complications.

I did not want it to be general knowledge. The last thing I wanted was to be shopping at the grocery store and have some person I hardly knew come and express his or her condolences. When I was out of the house in my daily routine, I just needed some normality to my life. I also had a number my friends at the time who were expecting babies, and I did not want them to feel like they could not discuss their excitement or their concerns in front of me because they felt it was cruel. The excitement of expecting a child is to be cherished, and I very much wanted to share in their excitement.

Yet even with those family and friends I had confided in, I withdrew. I didn't feel like going anywhere or doing anything. Not only was I continually tired and suffering from constant nausea, but I was also exhausted from the emotional roller-coaster I was on. I just wanted to be in my comfortable home, managing myself.

As I reflect on my own physical and mental state at the time, it may be helpful to make a few observations. I do this for the benefit of you, the reader, who may someday be in a position to support and help a person going through their own grief or hardship.

First, I freely recognise that I am a confident person. I don't like asking for help, and I enjoy doing most things myself. Until I became a mother, I had never been a particularly emotional person, and I was not prone to being anxious or fearful of anything much. My family and friends of course know this about me, and in fairness to them, it is easy to think that a confident person is doing just fine even in a tremendously difficult situation. It might be reasonable to conclude that every time you see confident people, they seem to be okay—their normal selves, so to speak—and therefore they must be coping.

I would like to recommend that you never make that assumption of anyone, especially of the confident ones. I myself have made the same assumptions of people. If they are not bawling their eyes out in front of me or heaven-forbid were even laughing in the face of dire circumstances, I would assume, "Surely everything is okay. They must be doing fine! Why bother saying anything? I won't bring it up. I don't want to make them sad."

Yes, I too have thought and done these things. However, I want to share with you what happens when the people who are close to you start acting this way. It seems to the suffering person as though their loved ones don't care. When you are suffering in the pit of grief, logic goes out of the window. It is not fair to expect people who are suffering so much to feel as though they are loved and supported if you are physically and practically not showing them any love and support. Logically they should know that you love them without you having to say it and that you will always be there for them. But it is in these hardships, in these times of grief and pain, that they need you to tell them and show them more than ever—continually.

I hear the argument that people don't want to keep bringing it up in conversation because they don't want to make you sad. And it is true, there are times when you would rather not discuss the situation or want to talk about something else. But if the topic is brought up, people always have the option of saying, "I can't talk about this now, but thanks for asking." However, if the question is never even asked, they never have that opportunity.

When family and close friends never broach the subject, never assure you of their love and support, never offer you any words of encouragement or kindness, and never tell you how much they are grieving for you, it makes your grief a very lonely place. Not only that, it distorts your view of how they are dealing with their grief for you and for themselves. Do they even care that they have a grandson/nephew/cousin, etc., who is going to pass away? Of course they do, but it is easy to think they don't, for what evidence is there to support that they feel this way? None.

Our family and friends were a really mixed bag. We had some who sent cards and notes to say they were thinking of us, cooked us meals, took us out for time-out, cried with us, prayed for us, phoned us to talk about the baby, sent us gifts, and asked us how we were doing regularly. We also had some who never mentioned the baby in front of us. It was never discussed. There was no word of encouragement given and no word of comfort offered. It was devastating.

We had some family members, both Christian and non-Christian, who, when we shared the news of the baby's condition, first asked, "So why didn't you get rid of it?" Wouldn't it be very easy to think that if people's initial reaction to the news is something like this, followed by months of no contact, no support, and no encouragement, that they actually don't care too much? Of course!

If you are ever in a situation to support people who are suffering, I want to encourage you to put your own awkwardness aside. Yes, it might be awkward to talk about the situation. It might even inconvenience you to make the call or take time to visit with, take them out for coffee, or offer to mind their children so they can have a bit of space. It might make you vulnerable, and it might make them vulnerable too. You may upset them, but unless you have been insensitive in how you have approached the subject (for example, asking a friend if they're "over it" yet in a public place), it is probably not you that is making them upset. It is the situation. And let's be honest, the situation is upsetting and it is good and right that they are upset. The worst they can do is tell you to bugger off. And even if they do, they will at least know that you cared enough to ask the question in the first place! At least they know that their suffering is important to you.

People who are suffering may not always open up to you when you seek to draw them out. They may not feel comfortable telling you all the ins and outs, or they may just not feel like it at the time. But I beg you, I implore you, don't let this be a reason to not ask! If they act in a way that is guarded from you, show them grace and understanding, and tell them that you are thinking of them and are there for them if they do ever want to talk.

If you are not comfortable telling people you are thinking of them, send a card. We have been very blessed by so many who have taken the time just to write us a quick note of encouragement, telling us they are thinking of us or praying for us. This has made all of the difference to us, and I encourage you to let your friend or family member know that you are thinking of him or her! It doesn't have to be more than that, but it should surely be no less than that.

As the weeks ticked by, we realised there were still so many unknowns about Stephen's condition. Dr Hart had been so encouraging. He had even given us his email address to contact him and ask questions or send him any information we thought would be relevant. Once again, we were blessed by his kindness towards us and the time he took to read and answer our questions.

We did some more legwork. We steadily gathered more information and testimonies, and we began to form a better idea of what life for little Stephen and us might look like.

Honestly, the complication that scared me the most was the possibility of horrendous facial deformities in an HPE baby. This was one of those moments where you wished you hadn't gone that extra click to "view image" online. My gut still wrenches at the thought of the image that was before me. It was a precious baby boy who had been born with Alobar HPE who had died immediately after birth. His mouth was a small hole in his forehead, and his nose was a single column too low for his face. His skin around his head fitted him poorly, as though it was a bandage that had been carelessly wrapped around his skull. This image is disturbing enough for anyone, but the thought that my baby might be born with such deformities was more than I could cope with.

I felt sick. For three full days, I felt physically ill because of the image. How would I cope if my boy was born like this? I knew I wanted to love and care for my baby as I would any of my children, but how would I cope looking into a face like that? I felt despair. I felt inadequate. My Stephen, no matter how he looked, was a precious gift from God. I knew it in my being, but I was so frightened.

As we studied and learned more about HPE, the practical implications of managing these complications began to hit home harder than they had before. We learned that there was a 25 per cent chance that Stephen might live anywhere between a few minutes up to six or so years of age.[xi] It was a far cry from the 99 per cent chance of dying within moments of birth we had been told repeatedly by each doctor. Up until this point, we had been given no hope whatsoever that Stephen would survive. We had been told he was unlikely to be born alive, and even if he was, he was unlikely to live more than a few moments. This was a whole new can of worms! Was I really looking at having to care for a child at home with special needs of this magnitude?

How was I going to cope with a baby who had to be peg fed? How was I going to cope with a baby who could not be trained into any sleeping pattern? How was I going to be able to drop everything to take him to the hospital if he had a sudden spike or drop of body temperature? How was I going to manage seizures? How was I going to give my two other beautiful children the care and love they needed when so much of my time would be spent caring for Stephen? The thought to me even now is still overwhelming. Oh, how I now have far more respect and admiration for those parents who care for children with special needs. You are truly amazing.

It was an incredibly unsettling time. I did not know what my future was going to look like. While we often pay lip service to the fact that we never really know what is going to happen in the next moment of our lives, for most of us, we have a general idea of where we are heading. We may know that unless something dramatic happens, we will have the same job twelve months from now. We know that we will probably be in the same house for the next five years. We will have finished our university course. We will be married and renovating our new home.

When you have a baby (particularly if it is not your first), you can mentally plan holidays and trips years in advance, knowing roughly what stage your child will be at. In fact, where children are involved, I was shocked to realise how much we subconsciously plan ahead and take things for granted. The new baby will be born, and we can carry on with family activities. We will go to playgroup. We will go to church. They will go to a certain school. For me, all of these things were totally unknown or out of the question.

I had no practical idea what my life would look like. So much of it depended on Stephen. Would he be born alive? Would he live for a few minutes, a few days, or many years? Would he be an unwell child, needing lots of attention, or would I be able to cope? Would I be able to go to church or to playgroup with my other kids and still manage? Would Michael be able to keep doing the job he was to support us? It was not until I began to be unsettled about all of these things that I realised how in many ways I had only paid lip service to Proverbs 27:1 which says, "Do not boast about tomorrow, for you do not know what a day may bring."

For the first time, I realised that planning for the future can be an idol. We look to our future plans as a measure of security rather than looking to God. Even if we are not putting our hope in financial wealth for security, we can still idolise the idea of what our future will be. The reality is, however, there are so many variables and influencing factors in our future that we can plan for it far less than what we care to admit. Just ask anyone who has lost his or her job or home as a result of the global financial crisis. Speak to someone who has been permanently disabled as a result of a transit accident. Ask someone who has lived through one of the natural disasters in recent years.

It had never before occurred to me that the fact we can plan ahead at all is actually a blessing. Furthermore, the fact that we can rely on Jesus to care for us regardless of how our plans work out is nothing short of grace. It has been a difficult lesson to learn, and I would not be truthful if I told you I was anxious for nothing during those months. For me, the uncertainty of my future was my biggest mental struggle of all. It played on my mind day and night. How often I had to be reminded that God was in control. Again and again I had to commit my situation to him in prayer, and each time I did, the pit of anxiety within me got a little less scary. It by no means went away completely, but I do distinctly remember getting to a point where, although I was hugely nervous about the future, I trusted God completely.

Philippians 4:13 says, "I can do all things through him who strengthens me." I clung to this verse with every fibre of my being, and God granted me his peace. This was a new revelation for me about God's peace. On some level, I think I had always assumed that God's peace was always a sort of blasé peace—an overwhelming sense of "everything is going to be okay," like some sort of emotional blanket of happiness.

I do believe that God offers this sort of blanket peace at times, but as I learned, we do not have to be happy or feeling good to experience his peace. I was uncertain about the future, and I was restless. I was not sleeping well, and thoughts churned in my mind day and night. But I was not despairing. God had it under control. He would give me the strength I needed for whatever task was before me. He would show me grace even in the times I failed miserably. His grace was sufficient for me, and in that knowledge, I had peace.

Ephesians 3:20–21 is another favourite verse of mine. It says:

> Now to him who is able to do far more
> abundantly than all that we ask or think,
> according to the power at work within
> us, to him be glory in the church and in
> Christ Jesus throughout all generations,
> forever and ever. Amen.

Do you know what happened as soon as I started to receive God's peace? He did more than I could have ever asked or thought to ask! He gave me hope. I was still nervous about bringing home a child with such a severe disability, but for the first time, I actually hoped it would happen. What a blessing it would be to be able to care for our son. If God would give me the strength and ability to cope, what an awesome privilege it would be to care for Stephen rather than something to be feared.

Suddenly, the future was not so bleak. In my mind, I saw Allison and Harry helping me care for their baby brother, feeding him, and cuddling him to sleep. I saw future family holidays differently. I imagined trips to the farm, trips to the beach, and trips to visit friends and family interstate and introducing them to our beautiful boy. Our hope was not in the certainty that any of these things would happen. Our hope was in the fact that we were Stephen's parents, and regardless of how long he lived, we would continue to have the privilege of being his parents. We were already rejoicing in the blessing of our son, and our hope was in the joy that he would continue to bring us, even if it meant challenges and strain.

It was interesting to me that a number of the non-Christians in our lives made comments to us about knowing that "our faith would get us through it." I wanted to correct them and tell them that it was not our faith that was getting us through it at all. My faith wavered so much; it was God who was carrying us.

I was also both curious and conscious of what the non-Christian members of our family thought about our decisions. I hated the idea that people assumed we were making decisions not to terminate or harm Stephen because it was against our religion, as if there were some sort of Christian rule-book that said we had to make certain choices. This fear was only exacerbated on one trip to the hospital where we shared a lift with a group of young girls after an apparent obstetrics appointment. The conversation went something like this:

> Girl 1: "Hmmmm, I'm not sure what to do now."
> Girl 2: "Yeah, it sucks. Hang on, though—you're a Catholic, aren't you?"
> Girl 1: "Yeah, I suppose so. But what does that have to do with it?"
> Girl 2: "Well, you can't get rid of it then. You're not allowed to. You'd be in so much trouble if you did that."

By using this example, I am not trying to judge the Catholic Church or their views (whatever they might actually be) about abortion. What I am trying to point out is how easy it is for people of any denomination—or any religious affiliation, for that matter—

to be stereotyped and even more sadly, feel they have to live up to that stereotype.

I can honestly say that we never once had a conversation with any other Christian about the rights and wrongs of termination. The decision was left to us, although I would like to think that if our decision had gone the other way, some of our loving friends may have stepped in to stop us from making a huge mistake. However, we never felt like we had to make this decision because we were Christians and this was what was expected of us. I seriously urge anyone who is feeling that way about any issue to prayerfully search out the Scriptures and enquire of God for your answer. If you don't, you are in danger of living a false Christian life based on rules and appearances, and you will never truly know the freedom you have in Christ. What a thing to miss out on.

Furthermore, it is a lesson to the rest of us in how we form judgments about other people. Perhaps we should do less assuming about people and why they do what they do and more asking. Even if we think we know the answer, we should challenge each other in our loving, close relationships as to what is motivating us. This type of accountability requires an enormous amount of trust and mutual respect in the relationship, but it is the very essence of a godly friendship.

I am so grateful for the godly friend I have in my husband. The uncertainty about our future was still there. Michael and I fluctuated constantly. From day to day we would change our minds as to whether we thought it would be better for Stephen and for us if he passed away soon after birth or if we were able to bring him home. There were many pros to both scenarios. It was truly one of those times when we had no idea what the best outcome would be. Even until the day of Stephen's birth, we had no idea what outcome we wanted.

In many ways, it was a totally freeing place to be. We had no preference; we were totally at God's mercy and glad to be.

Romans 8:28 says: "We know that in all things God works for good with those who love him, those whom he has called according to his purpose" (GNT).

What a promise! What joy! We were able to entrust our uncertain future to a God who would bring about the best possible outcome for us and for Stephen! We had peace, hope, and joy in the midst of grief and suffering. Only our God can do that!

5

A Study in Psalm 139

It is difficult for me to describe where my head and heart were while we were waiting for the birth of our son. We had the underlying peace of God and trust in him to help us, but I was still terrified at the selfishness of my own being. I did not trust myself to be able to make godly decisions, and even though I trusted God to help me, I was still scared of making the wrong choice. Some people may call this a lack of faith. Some may call this an immature faith. Regardless of what you call it, that's how it was.

During those weeks, we received a beautiful card from friends of ours. They sent us encouragement and comfort for the times we were facing. At the bottom of the card was a Bible reference—Psalm 139. Verses from Psalm 139 had kept coming across our path in recent weeks, but I don't think I had yet sat down and read the entire chapter. Now as I've said before, I am no theologian, but I would like to share with you some of the things God revealed to me as I read and re-read this Psalm. To save you the trouble of looking it up, here it is:

> O LORD, you have searched me and known me! You know when I sit down and when I rise up; you discern my thoughts from afar. You search out my path and my lying down and are

acquainted with all my ways. Even before a word is on my tongue, behold, O LORD, you know it altogether. You hem me in, behind and before, and lay your hand upon me. Such knowledge is too wonderful for me; it is high; I cannot attain it. Where shall I go from your Spirit? Or where shall I flee from your presence? If I ascend to heaven, you are there! If I make my bed in Sheol, you are there! If I take the wings of the morning and dwell in the uttermost parts of the sea, even there your hand shall lead me, and your right hand shall hold me. If I say, "Surely the darkness shall cover me, and the light about me be night," even the darkness is not dark to you; the night is bright as the day, for darkness is as light with you. For you formed my inward parts; you knitted me together in my mother's womb. I praise you, for I am fearfully and wonderfully made. Wonderful are your works; my soul knows it very well. My frame was not hidden from you, when I was being made in secret, intricately woven in the depths of the earth. Your eyes saw my unformed substance; in your book were written, every one of them, the days that were formed for me, when as yet there was none of them. How precious to me are your thoughts, O God! How vast is the sum of them! If I would count them,

> they are more than the sand. I awake, and I am still with you. Oh that you would slay the wicked, O God! O men of blood, depart from me! They speak against you with malicious intent; Your enemies take your name in vain! Do I not hate those who hate you, O LORD? And do I not loathe those who rise up against you? I hate them with complete hatred; I count them my enemies. *Search me, O God, and know my heart! Try me and know my thoughts! And see if there be any grievous way in me, and lead me in the way everlasting!* (emphasis mine).

The first part that struck me in this Psalm was the last two verses (emphasized above). God had given me a prayer straight from the scriptures to help me trust him in my decision making. I prayed these verses many times each day. It was an awesome reminder to me to keep seeking God wholeheartedly about every aspect of Stephen's life and to test all my thoughts and emotions against his Word. There is a particular verse from Hebrews that demonstrates this beautifully:

> For the word of God is living and active, sharper than any two-edged sword, piercing to the division of soul and of spirit, of joints and of marrow, and discerning the thoughts and intentions of the heart (Heb. 4:12).

We know that the Bible is God's living Word, and so the task before Michael and me was to test our thoughts and emotions against the Scripture. I must be honest and say that I actively pursued this on some days more than others. There were many times my emotions and my fatigue got the better of me and I just went about my day asking God to carry me through it.

When we considered Stephen's life and our journey as his parents in the light of Psalm 139, we were reassured of many things we had already felt. I will work through the main points of the Psalm and what God was saying to us through them.

> O LORD, you have searched me and
> known me! You know when I sit down
> and when I rise up; you discern my
> thoughts from afar. You search out my
> path and my lying down and are
> acquainted with all my ways. Even
> before a word is on my tongue, behold,
> O LORD, you know it altogether. You
> hem me in, behind and before, and lay
> your hand upon me. Such knowledge is
> too wonderful for me; it is high; I cannot
> attain it.

God knew the decisions we were going to make—right or wrong—ahead of time, and he had planned for them. We still needed to seek him and honour him with every intention of our being, but he was in control of the situation, and his grace and favour were towards us.

Not only was he in control of the situation, but he was also moving people around us to love and support us. I remember one day not long after Stephen was diagnosed, a godly man who is a real prayer warrior from our church (who incidentally is old enough to be my grandfather) sent me an email to ask me if everything was okay. He did not know about Stephen's condition at that stage, but in his prayer times, the Lord had shown him that our family needed extra prayer and support at the moment, although he didn't know why. How it makes my soul rejoice each time I think about this. God was moving in the hearts of others to love us and support us even before they knew anything was wrong. What a wonderful example of hemming us in, behind and before.

> Where shall I go from your Spirit? Or where shall I flee from your presence? If I ascend to heaven, you are there! If I make my bed in Sheol, you are there! If I take the wings of the morning and dwell in the uttermost parts of the sea, even there your hand shall lead me, and your right hand shall hold me.

God would not leave us; he was always there to help us. Even in the times when the grief was so great and we were so emotionally numb that we did not feel he was with us, he was.

> If I say, "Surely the darkness shall cover me, and the light about me be night," even the darkness is not dark to you; the night is bright as the day, for darkness is as light with you.

Even in this time of hardship and grief, we could glorify God for his gift of Stephen, the privilege of being Stephen's parents, the awesome miracle of life, and the promises of help. This situation was not dark to God. Stephen was made by God for His glory. God was to be glorified because Stephen was safely in his hands, both now and after he would pass away.

> Your eyes saw my unformed substance;
> in your book were written, every one of
> them, the days that were formed for me,
> when as yet there was none of them.

God knew how long Stephen would be with us. He had perfectly planned every day. What comfort and joy it brought us to know that God knew the plan he had for Stephen exactly and that we were allowed to be a part of the plan! God brought about the events of Stephen's life in a way that was best for Stephen, for Michael, and for myself.

> How precious to me are your thoughts, O
> God! How vast is the sum of them! If I
> would count them, they are more than
> the sand. I awake, and I am still with you.

God's plan for Stephen and for us was so much more than we could imagine. Even then we trusted that God would touch people's lives though Stephen's and through ours in ways we could not fathom. Stephen's life was no accident, and it would not be in vain.

> Oh that you would slay the wicked, O
> God! O men of blood, depart from me!
> They speak against you with malicious
> intent; Your enemies take your name in
> vain! Do I not hate those who hate you,
> O LORD? And do I not loathe those who
> rise up against you? I hate them with
> complete hatred; I count them my
> enemies.

We must stand our ground against those who do not honour God—against those who sought to end Stephen's life or cause him harm. God gave us awesome responsibility as Stephen's parents, and we were not to give in and conform to the world around us.

You may have noticed there was a small section of the Psalm that I skipped. I have saved this for last because this was the most difficult part for me to fathom. In fact, I truly came unstuck when I reflected on these words:

> For you formed my inward parts; you knitted me together in my mother's womb. I praise you, for I am fearfully and wonderfully made. Wonderful are your works; my soul knows it very well.

Until I stopped to reflect on this Scripture, I had subconsciously and wrongly concluded something about God. I knew God is the author of all life and that Stephen was a gift from him. I also knew that it was because of the fall of man that Stephen suffered from the condition he did. With these two facts, I therefore concluded that Stephen was actually not as he should be—that God had just allowed this result of the curse to occur, but he loved Stephen anyway and was going to bless him and others through him.

You may see the problem with my poor theology. The verses above don't say, "You let me come together in my mother's womb, and I am formed as a result of a genetic defect." No! The Scripture says Stephen was knit together! He was fearfully and wonderfully made! This was no accident. This was not unplanned by God.

But how could this be? It was far easier for me to hold onto my belief that "God is good and only gives good gifts to his children" if I believed that Stephen just happened to be like this as a result of a genetic accident and God was going to mop up the mess one way or another. But how could a God who is good and loving deliberately make Stephen this way? Why would he do that? How could he be purposeful in creating a child who was going to suffer so much?

I was stuck. I honestly did not understand what "fearfully made" actually meant. I remember looking through various translations at the time. I even looked up the passage in my limited range of study Bibles and concordances, and every one of them seemed to conveniently gloss over the topic.

Honestly, it was not until just now when I sat to write this book that I was given some insight into this Scripture. At the time, Michael and I searched online to see if any of my favourite preachers had any sermons or resources on the topic, desperate for an answer. It was then we came across an awesome sermon written by John Piper entitled "Why Was This Child Born Blind?"[xii]

For anyone who is facing circumstances of illness or disability from birth, I can't recommend this sermon highly enough. John Piper examines the passage from John 9:1–23 about the man who was born blind and the Pharisees who were divided once Jesus healed the man. The key verses in this passage (on this subject, at least) are verses 1 through 3, which say:

> As he passed by, he saw a man blind
> from birth. And his disciples asked him,
> "Rabbi, who sinned, this man or his
> parents, that he was born blind?" Jesus
> answered, "It was not that this man
> sinned, or his parents, but that the works
> of God might be displayed in him.

Is it possible that God not only allowed the defect that caused the man to be blind from birth to happen but was actually purposeful in doing so? And to what end? Was it so God's glory might be shown through him?

I'm not going to lie—this can be a difficult truth to digest. The harder God's truth is to digest usually correlates with how highly we have elevated ourselves in our own minds. If we take the stance, "How could God allow this to happen to me and my child?" we have forgotten that we are in fact *not* God. We are not the author of life.

The only reason we are even here is because we have been created and had life breathed into us by God. We had no say in our own existence, and even our parents played only a very small part. Every single particle of our being was formed in such a miraculous way that even science can only explain so much. John Macarthur sums this up beautifully when he remarks, "As Christians we accept one big miracle—God—one big miracle—God—and everything else makes sense. An atheist denies God and has to have a miracle for every other thing."[xiii]

To say that God just allowed Stephen's deformity to happen without any real plan is poor theology indeed. Pastor Piper puts it this way:

> God knows all things. He knows exactly what is happening in the moment of conception. When there is a defective chromosome or some genetic irregularity in the sperm that is about to fertilize an egg, God can simply say no. He commands the winds. He commands the waves. He commands the sperm and the genetic makeup of the egg. If God foresees and permits a conception that

he knows will produce blindness, he has reasons for this permission. And those reasons are his purposes. His designs. His plans. God never has met a child from whom he had no plan. There are no accidents in God's mind or hands. And secondly, any attempt to deny God's sovereign, wise, purposeful control over conception and birth has a head-on collision with Exodus 4:11 and Psalm 139:13. "The Lord said to Moses, 'Who has made man's mouth? Who makes him mute, or deaf, or seeing, or blind? Is it not I, the Lord?'" "You formed my inward parts; you knitted me together in my mother's womb."[xiv]

How I have since loved that passage from Exodus 4:11. It has been my constant companion throughout my journey with Stephen. God did make Stephen, and he made him exactly how he wanted him so that his glory might be shown. Many choose to look at hardship and suffering as being cruel and unfair—as though we are owed something more. But God owes us nothing. We are here in whatever capacity he has ordained for us, and it is a blessing that we even exist. If we did not exist, we would not have the chance to experience love, friendship, laughter, marriage, or parenthood. If we did not exist, we would not have the opportunity to know our heavenly Father, which is truly the most awesome privilege we have. We know the Maker of the universe, and what's more, we can call him Father! It does not get any better than that!

When our minds start to grasp this concept—and we can only begin to—an astounding and humbling awe enters us. God is awesome, and we are totally at his mercy. That alone is truly terrifying. God not only loves us with perfect love, but 1 John 4:8 also says *he is love!* It is an incredible juxtaposition to being truly terrifying. It is terrifying to think that we are entirely at the mercy of God, yet we can trust him totally and completely because he loves us so utterly and can always be trusted to do what is best for us. This is the fear of the Lord! It is terrifying and wonderful all at the same time. No wonder David says we are fearfully and wonderfully made! I think the Amplified Bible puts Psalm 139:14 best:

> I will confess and praise You for You are fearful and wonderful and for the awful wonder of my birth! Wonderful are Your works, and that my inner self knows right well.

If we had not had Stephen, I would have never had the same opportunity to learn these things about God and have it affect me deeply in the way it has. I would not have the capacity for love that I now do. I would not have the same living proof that I now have to share with others that God is faithful to his promises and to his children. God has given us so many opportunities to trust him so we can show those around us that God is to be trusted, praised, glorified, respected, honoured, and worshipped, even in the most difficult of situations. I would not have the ability to sympathise and not just empathise with God in what it must have felt like for him to see his own Son, Jesus, die.

In many ways, Stephen had the best deal in all of this. He was unaware of the complexities of his creation. He was cared for and loved as much as any baby could be. He did suffer, but his suffering was cut short, and he now is walking and leaping with Jesus in heaven—a place where I long to be!

6

The Wall

Things had been progressing as expected with Stephen's development. I had finally made up my mind that Stephen was going to be born full term and that he was so healthy we would probably bring him home from the hospital. I had been reluctant to take any steps towards getting Stephen's bedroom ready until now because I didn't think I could face the heartbreak of having a nursery that would never be used. But now I was sure. Things were going well. I knew we would be bringing Stephen home, so I bought some wall stickers to decorate his nursery, and Allison, Harry, and I set about getting Stephen's room ready for him. We had a joyous time together, making it special for him.

Of course, later that week we hit a bump in the road—a big one. Stephen's head was measuring the size of a thirty-two-week-old baby on the ultrasound, slightly larger than was to be expected. This is a fact that would not raise too much concern in an otherwise-healthy baby. However, judging by the uneasiness in my obstetrician's face, I was missing something. As it turns out, the complication of HPE babies having too much fluid in their heads where the brain is supposed to be is not just a complication that happens post-birth. It is also a common problem in utero.

All of a sudden, we were facing potential complications we had never even considered. If Stephen's head was growing fast, he would have to be born by the time his head reached the size it should be at forty weeks' gestation to avoid complications at birth. We would have to closely monitor his head size.

Another week passed by, and Stephen's head had grown rapidly. His head was now measuring at thirty-four weeks' size at only thirty-one weeks of gestation. This was not a good sign.

True to form, my obstetrician announced that if it were him, he would arrange to have the baby induced immediately. Obviously he still did not understand me. There was no added danger to myself in waiting until Stephen's head was at least full term size, but there was plenty for Stephen if we delivered early. The doctor thought I should have terminated Stephen's life when he was first diagnosed, and his view had obviously not changed. The doctor's philosophy was, "Get him out, over, and done with, because there is no hope or value in his life."

The doctor then informed us that the drugs they would need to use to induce at such an early age of gestation would probably kill the baby anyway. When I pointed out to him that under the circumstances, that was actually no different from deliberately terminating his life at twenty weeks, he could see there was no point in arguing with me. He then concluded the conversation by telling me it was a relief for him to refer me back to the larger hospital to manage Stephen's birth.

Thanks, Doc. I'm so glad you are feeling more comfortable about the situation.

So, back to the specialist hospital I trotted, and by the time I made my first appointment, Stephen's head was measuring at thirty-six weeks. We were now at only thirty-two weeks of gestation.

Michael and I were in a spin. We had been thinking we had almost two months before things would happen in any practical sense, yet here we were facing the possibility of our son being born early—way early.

When the hospital recognised the potential situation, we were allotted a consultation with one of the obstetricians on staff to discuss a plan. First the doctor explained to us that when Stephen's head reached forty weeks in size, we would need to act so as to not cause any unnecessary complications for the birth. This made sense to us. He then went on to explain that they would try to induce me into labour.

Wait. We were told that the drugs used to induce labour at such an early stage were likely to kill Stephen. When I asked the obstetrician about this, the response was, "Oh, it is possible but not likely." Hmmmm. Who to believe? I was starting to get a sinking feeling.

What about the fact the baby was still in breech position? Wasn't that going to add complications? As it turned out, they had an answer for everything. The doctor said, "We can perform a decompression." As soon as the word was mentioned, it rang alarm bells. I remembered one of the radiographers talking about this at the last ultrasound. I didn't remember much about what he said, but what I had remembered didn't sound all that great, especially since he mentioned that such a procedure was likely to stop baby's heart.

We asked the doctor to more fully explain this procedure to us. As it turned out, in this scenario a decompression would mean inserting a needle into Stephen's skull to remove excess fluid from his head. This would be performed if his head became stuck during labour. The mental image of having a half-born baby with arms and legs already out and having a needle stuck into his skull while he was still lodged inside me made me sick to my stomach. The thought of inflicting such a painful procedure on my son was heartbreaking. Worse than that was the risk they were suggesting we take in stopping Stephen's heart.

I told the doctor that we were not keen on the procedure because we had been told previously that such a procedure was

The Wall

likely to stop baby's heart. Again, the answer he gave was that it was "unlikely."

Interesting. Now we had conflicting information on two different procedures, and the fact that this doctor did not seem interested in preserving Stephen's life did not give me a lot of faith in his answers. What should we do? Who could we trust? If we were to ask for a second opinion, the likelihood of another doctor who would be inclined to persuade us towards painful or unnecessary procedures for our son based on so-called odds was high. We didn't feel like there was anyone we could trust, and we were both so exhausted at the constant resistance we were getting from doctors that it was too hard to think of where we might be able to get some reliable information.

I told the doctor then and there I was not comfortable with the idea of either the decompression or the induction because both seemed to put our baby at unnecessary risk. I explained that this baby was as precious to us as any of our other kids, and we would not do anything to unnecessarily put him in harm's way. More than that, we were not going to inflict any harm or pain upon him unless there was absolutely no other option.

It was almost as if I saw a wall go up. There was no look of recognition or understanding on his face. I asked the doctor why a caesarean section could not be performed. He told us that it would be a completely unnecessary risk to me—the mother—and that he would not even consider it until all other avenues had been exhausted.

My mind reeled. How could this be? In Australia, it is estimated that between 8,500 and 12,400 elective caesareans are performed every year.[xv] Why was the doctor being so difficult about performing a caesarean? I asked the doctor if having the caesarean would put me at any greater risk than any other healthy mother having the same procedure, and he confirmed there was no greater risk.

I asked, "So why? Why would you deny it to me?"

I sincerely hope the answer he gave us makes you as angry as it made me. I could not believe what I heard. "Stephen has a 99.9 per cent chance of not surviving very long after he is born, and his life is not worth risking complications to you."

So let me get this straight. There are women who can elect to have caesareans in this country just because they do not want to endure the pain of childbirth. There are women who elect to have caesareans whose children are at far less risk than what my child would be in having life-threatening drugs coursing through his system or a large needle inserted into his skull. In spite of all this, the doctor was willing to risk my baby's life because he did not deem Stephen's life to be at all valuable, in spite of his parent's pleas to value his life as any other child.

And what about that statistic—that Stephen had a 99.9 per cent chance of passing away moments after childbirth? There is a made-up statistic if ever I heard one. Even when I tried to point out that the credible medical research papers on the subject suggested there was actually a 25 per cent chance of him surviving anywhere up to six years, he looked at us as with incredulity.[xvi] He obviously thought we had false hope for our baby. He was the expert. What would two emotionally involved simpletons like us know?

The obstetrician was unmoved. He suggested that we go home, think about the options, and understand that a caesarean would only be considered as an absolute last resort.

I was ready to explode. He did not comprehend that it didn't matter to us whether or not Stephen only lived a few moments or much longer after birth—no matter what happened, we did not want to harm him. We thought perhaps we could persuade the doctor to change his mind if we called in a paediatrician to verify what we had learned about life expectancy, so we requested that the on-duty paediatrician come to speak with us. What a mistake.

The Wall

To this day I am not sure whether the doctor spoke to the paediatrician before he met with us to ensure we were convinced there was no hope. What I do know is that our experience with the paediatrician was the rudest, most inconsiderate, and most arrogant encounter I have ever had with a doctor.

The paediatrician walked into the room. "Tell me why I'm here," was his opening line. "I don't even know why I am here. There is no hope for your baby."

I saw the anger rise up in Michael's face, and it mirrored my own internal emotion. "You are here," I began, "to tell us what sort of support would be offered to an otherwise healthy baby who would be born at thirty-four weeks."

"Why do you ask this question? It is irrelevant. There will be no support offered to your son. There is no point."

"What if the only help he needs is some oxygen to help him breathe?"

"No. None. There is a 99.9 per cent chance of your baby dying right after he is born. It is likely that he will just gurgle a little and then die. I won't even be present at his birth; there is no point."

I don't know what made me angrier—that false statistic being rammed down my throat again as justification to not care for our son or the fact that he was being so overwhelmingly rude.

Then there was the clincher—his closing statement. "Better luck next time."

When the paediatrician left the room, we cried. This wall was insurmountable. No doctor at this hospital cared for our baby or had shown us any compassion. Not one. It shouldn't have been any great surprise to us that a staff member entered less than two minutes later with a printed birth plan for Stephen upon the recommendation of the paediatrician, which included no intervention after the baby was born. Now I type at roughly ninety-six words per minute, and I would have struggled to get a document like that prepared in such a short time. Clearly the fate of our baby had already been discussed and decided beforehand, without reference to our views on the subject. To this day, I believe those doctors conspired to ensure that no hope was given to us for the birth of our son and that no ground would be given on their part for his post-natal care.

We went home shattered. It was another week until our next appointment, and the doctor suggested that it would be a good time to think over our "options." I have never been so unsettled in my life. Not only was there the emotional turmoil of losing our son, but there was also the frustration of not being heard or understood and the added fight for the wellbeing of our son. We were both exhausted. It shouldn't be this way. We should not have to fight so hard for his life. You see, every doctor seemed to make a false equation about the value of life, and if I had to express it as a mathematical equation, it would look something like this: $V = Q$, where V is "value of life" and Q is "quality of life."

Our son was going to be severely handicapped. If he did live, he would never progress beyond the physical or mental capacity of a newborn baby. He would never be able to sit up. He would never be able to feed or eat like a normal child. He would most likely have no recognition of who we were as his parents because he would likely have no memory. He would have no capacity to learn anything, including the ability to develop his motor skills. Yet his life meant just as much to us as any of our children. We wanted the opportunity to help him, to love him, and to serve him as parents. He would always be loved and cared for. He was already a cherished member of our family. His happiness and well-being did not revolve around what he could and could not do.

As I thought about our situation, I considered some of the people I know who are disabled, some from birth and some who have become unwell or injured during their lives. Do they experience frustration, suffering, and hardship? Absolutely! But do they consider their lives to be any less valuable than anyone else's? Of course not! In fact, it has been my observation that many handicapped people enjoy life more fully than those who are fully able-bodied because they *don't* take the abilities they have for granted. They live life and enjoy life within the capacity they have. To say that the value of life equates to the quality of life is a poor equation indeed.

I know a mother who has a son who suffers from autism and ADHD. She has written a book about her and her son's journey with autism, and she provides this honest insight into living with disability:

> Why is it such a big deal to have a child who isn't typical or normal? Why does every prospective parent say, "I don't mind what it is, just as long as it's healthy…?" Why do we all secretly cringe when we see someone who is disabled or challenged or disturbed?
>
> I have spent the last two or three months feeling sad, heavy and dismayed by the idea that my child is going to struggle in life with his understanding and communication. But in stopping to analyse the fears I have for him, I can see that I'm most afraid of other people's reactions to him. I'm worried that he'll be bullied, excluded, laughed at, tormented or just plain ignored.

> How do I know he will suffer these things? Because I know my own heart, and I know my own sinful reactions to others who are different from me. I have bullied, excluded, laughed at, tormented and just plain ignored people who were 'imperfect'.
>
> And in doing so, I have shown my own imperfections, which are far more serious, far more deadly and far more vile than any physical or mental disability could ever be. The real human imperfection is the sinful, unloving heart that each one of us carries inside.
>
> If we humans were truly able to love, having a disabled child would not be a cause of sorrow. It might create a few extra challenges, but parents would not fear for their children, and societies would care for them.
>
> Perhaps the 'imperfect people' are part of the world in order to show up everybody else's imperfection.
>
> Cecily Paterson
> *Love, Tears & Autism*, 2011[xvii]

As we prayed and considered during that week, we knew that we were unmoved in our initial stance. We could not put Stephen's life in unnecessary danger, and we would not

The Wall

unnecessarily inflict harm or hurt upon him. The one thing I did concede, however, was that if Stephen had turned around and was no longer in breech position (i.e., engaged), I would go ahead with an induction as long as his head was not larger than full term. The possibility of Stephen's head becoming stuck was far higher if he was induced while he was in breech position. The doctor had convinced me that the medication they would use to induce me was no different than what would be used at a full-term induction. Having had two children previously, one of which was induced, I felt this was a reasonable decision.

With our minds made up, we went for another check with the doctor. By this stage, Stephen was at thirty-three weeks, and his head was at forty weeks—full term. We knew action would need to be taken soon. In fact, I packed a small bag that day with the hope that they might even act.

The waiting had been killing me. I couldn't sleep. All I could think about every moment of every day was our precious son being born and having a better idea of how the next few weeks/months of our lives were going to look. My hopes weren't high that the doctors were going to act then and there, but I was going prepared.

With painful casualness, the doctor met with us to confirm the results of the scan we had just had. Stephen's head was at full-term size, but the good news was he was now engaged. The time was drawing close where we would need to act.

He asked if we had considered the options from the previous appointment, and by God's grace, we stood firm. We told him we were uncomfortable with the decompression procedure, but since Stephen's head was now engaged, we would consent to an induction. It came as no surprise to us that the doctor agreed on this course of action, and we were told to return to the hospital on Tuesday. Today was Thursday.

I was annoyed at the lack of understanding the doctor was showing. It really did not seem to hit home the urgency of our situation. While I do understand that elective inductions and procedures must be scheduled to manage the hospital's resources, it was the lack of empathy that grated against me. He and his staff did not seem to grasp that unlike most births, it was not only the anticipation of our baby's birth that was causing our stress but the fact that it was also likely to be the time when our son would pass away. That amount of mental stress is almost unbearable.

   Nevertheless, we put it in our minds that Tuesday was the day. There was an end in sight. It was the most painful waiting I have ever done. To help pass the excruciating weekend, we had dinner with good friends on the Saturday night before the induction. I am not sure how I held it together. All I can say is I am grateful for God's grace in keeping me together throughout those days, and I am grateful for such wonderful friends. Many of our family and friends were empathetic towards our situation, but I knew these friends got it. This was enough to get us through that weekend.

7

The Arrival

*A*s soon as I woke up, it was in my head. I have spent more than twenty-five years of my life studying music, singing in choirs, and performing. After so many years of training, I seem to be able to recall lyrics of hundreds of songs with relative ease. My memory in other areas is not so flash, but I can remember every Latin word to Vivaldi's "Gloria," which I have not sung since I was in primary school.

It was not the first time I have felt God use this ability in me to speak to me. That morning when I woke up, the first thing that was in my head were lyrics to an old chorus I had not thought about for at least fifteen years. The lyrics from this chorus are taken from Deuteronomy 32:2b-4:

> Ascribe greatness to our God!
> "The Rock, his work is perfect,
> for all his ways are justice.
> A God of faithfulness and
> without iniquity,
> just and upright is he.

What comfort those words gave me. I had a peculiar peace. I was so grateful to God for reminding me of these things. I knew he was in control, and I knew everything that was about to happen was his perfect work. I did not need to worry.

Oh, how in the days to follow I would desperately need to remember this. We arrived at the hospital first thing in the morning, bags packed and expectations high. We had thought today was the day. When we saw the doctor, he had no concrete plans. In fact, it seemed as though he was ready to send us home. This was not a great start.

After some pleading on our part, he decided to see if there was a bed for us. Thankfully there was, although we would have to wait several hours. We decided to go to the local shopping mall and catch a movie while we waited. We were happy; our son was going to be born later that day. There was a lot to look forward to.

The movie was absolute rubbish, but it didn't matter. I remember having a wonderful, fun time with my husband. The gravity of the moment was not lost on either of us. This was it. This was special time we got to spend together before our lives were about to be changed. We rejoiced in the excitement of the birth of our son, and we rejoiced in the love and friendship in our marriage. God was indeed good.

Our arrival back to the hospital at the appointed time saw me ushered into a private room. I was really glad for a private room. The thought that I might have a baby who had passed away yet have to share a room with a happy mother and her baby was too cruel. I'm glad someone at the hospital finally saw some sense.

It was not long before the first course of treatment commenced. Any woman who has been induced will likely know the standard procedure. Gel was applied to my cervix. As I mentioned earlier, I had been induced once before when I gave birth to my son Harry. I was induced at forty weeks, and he had been born within eight hours of the gel being applied, so our expectations were high. We thought we would be holding our beautiful boy before the night was out.

The Arrival

I felt somewhat uncomfortable in the hours that followed—some mild contractions but not the contractions I had been anticipating. Well, I concluded, you can't expect every birth to be the same. After six hours, a new on-duty doctor appeared to apply the second course of gel. Hmmm. I was not expecting this. The doctor soon explained that three applications of gel at six-hour intervals was considered a single course of treatment. This would put me well into the night. But what choice did I have? They administered the next course of treatment and left Michael and me to endure the next six hours.

It was painful in every sense. It was uncomfortable no matter what position I was in, but it was not labour. I couldn't sleep. I was tired and sore. By the time they came in at 2:00 a.m. to apply the third dose of gel, I was well and truly over it. Not only was I sick of having a different and unfamiliar doctor invading my personal lady-space on a six-hourly rotation, nothing was happening. My husband slept peacefully beside me in the foldout bed on the floor, and I was smouldering. My anxiety over Stephen's life, the pain I was experiencing, and the lack of sleep was a bad combination.

On the bright side, Michael and I had concluded that now they would have no option but to give me the caesarean because the induction had failed. When my obstetrician arrived in the room the next morning, I was less than cordial. He was lucky to escape the room alive, however, when he then announced that standard procedure was that they would now rest my body for twelve hours and administer another full course of gel.

What!

This had never been explained to us! I could not think of anything worse. I was in pain. I was exhausted. I was anxious. We were already supposed to have had our baby. This was not on the cards. In hindsight, I realise that our expectations of induction were far too high. However, I place the blame for this squarely on the

81

doctor's shoulders. It had never been explained to us that induction at thirty-four weeks can often take days. It was a massive shock to learn that it might be another day or so until we had our son.

The tension was unbearable, and after he left the room, I had the biggest meltdown of my life. I am not exaggerating. I am usually a fairly controlled person—not overly emotional or prone to fits of anger in public—but I was so distraught that I could not even stand straight. I cried. No, I bawled. I sobbed uncontrollably like a woman who has just been told that her husband has been killed in some freak accident.

I'll tell them where to stick their gel! Even in my distress, the irony of that thought did not escape me. But I had had enough. My husband was despairing. He did not know how to help me. Had I not been so utterly tender from the gel, I honestly believe I would have gone on a rampage through the maternity ward and given every staff member a piece of my mind. I felt out of control, and it was horrible. I have never felt like that before in my life.

After about twenty minutes of having an absolute meltdown, I started to calm down. I decided to have a shower, and as I stood there sobbing and letting the warm streams of water drizzle down my pregnant belly, I cried to God. "Lord, I am at the end of my tether. I don't want to have more treatment. Every fibre of my being is against it." As I cried, those words came back into my mind: "His work is perfect, and all His ways are just."

I pondered this for a while. I knew he wanted me to trust him. He knew this was going to happen ahead of time, and he had the situation under control. As I accepted this, I began to calm down, and for the first time, I contemplated agreeing to the second course of gel. I was by no means certain that I would agree, but it was an enormous step. I had gone from total meltdown to seeing reason within half an hour, and I thank God for his reassurance in those moments.

The Arrival

I emerged from the shower and related to Michael what had just happened. Satisfied I was not about to tear the maternity ward apart, Michael agreed to go and spend some time at home with our children since it had been the better part of two days since they had seen us. I asked him to come back for the evening and spend the night by my side, which he gladly agreed to.

So there I was, by myself, waiting, and still fuming on some level. This was not how I had pictured it. By this time, I should have been cuddling my baby boy and introducing him to his brother and sister. I was so frustrated at the doctors. Why hadn't they explained this? They seemed to have little care that resting for another twelve hours followed by potentially another eighteen hours of painful treatment was as good as torture in my current physical and mental state.

Ever since I had been admitted to hospital, the nursing staff kept offering to send a social worker to visit with me. Up until this point, I had declined. I was a strong woman, and I felt sure there was nothing the social worker could offer me to help my situation. Even in the depths of my frustration, I still didn't want to see a social worker, so it ticked me off somewhat that even though I had repeatedly declined, the nursing staff sent one to my room anyway.

In hindsight I wish even more that they had respected my wishes and not sent her. She caught me at a time of extreme distress, and I blurted out my frustrations to her from start to present and how I just wished that the doctors would listen to me. I also told her I was seriously considering turning down the second course of gel to force their hand to do something more practical.

Unfortunately, instead of keeping her thoughts to herself, she decided that sharing them with me was the way to go. I wish she hadn't. She said, "Well, Hannah, I want you to know that I totally understand where you are coming from. I can see that with everything you are experiencing, your distress is perfectly reasonable under the circumstances. My only concern is that if you start refusing medical treatment, the staff members on the ward are going to start thinking you have mental issues."

Mental issues! *Mental issues!* I was totally shattered, worse than before. Not only was I in the most distraught state of my life, but the rug had been completely pulled out from under me. I felt that no matter what I did from that point forward, no one would take me seriously. I already felt the doctors were not listening to me, but to think that the nursing staff would now ignore anything I had to say was too much. Emotionally, I was worse than before.

I have since spoken to doctors, nursing staff, and another social worker about this incident in an infant loss clinic many weeks after the event, and they were all deeply horrified that this was said to me at such a moment. Even if this was a genuine concern of the social worker at the time, she should never have told me that. She should have kept it to herself or had a quiet word with the nursing staff. Furthermore, everyone I have spoken to has refuted her suggestion that the nursing staff would have viewed me as having mental issues. One of the midwives from the same ward later said to me, "That is the last thing they would have thought. If anything, they would have been just as distressed for you."

So here I was—distraught once again. Alone. Unheard. Untrusting. By the time the hour came for the second course of treatment to begin, I agreed. I felt as if I had no choice. I couldn't bear the thought of people thinking I was mentally unstable and not taking me seriously, especially when I needed such help. But I knew God was in control. He had seen everything that had happened. This was all a part of his plan. Michael sat by my side and held my hand as they began the treatment. When they left the room, he prayed with me.

As the hours ticked on, I became more and more uncomfortable. I agreed to a dose of sleeping tablets I had refused the night before. I was exhausted. I didn't feel like this second course of gel was going to make much difference, so what did it

The Arrival

matter if I was in a deep sleep? I felt sure this baby wouldn't be coming, regardless of how much gel they applied.

It was a great decision. I slept well and only woke when I changed position because of my discomfort. The doctors woke me in the early hours of the morning to administer the second course of gel. The signs were not good. This unfamiliar face who was examining my lady-parts confirmed that there was no real progress and they would check with my doctor first thing in the morning as to how to proceed.

Morning came, and although I had slept, I was totally finished. This was it. I knew I was due for one last application of gel, but I said to Michael that I was going to refuse it. I was so sore, and I was not satisfied that there was significant progress. They were going to have to move on.

In my mind, the next step was a caesarean section. I already understood that it might be another day or so before this could happen, depending on theatre schedules, but that was okay. If I knew there was a definite resolution in the works, I could cope.

It would seem however, our expectations were once again unrealistic. Without my having to refuse treatment, the doctors had already decided that my progress was not sufficient and they would not administer the sixth dose of gel. I was grateful—that is, until I heard what the next course of action was to be.

A new doctor was sent in, one I had never met before. Michael and I sat in horror as he conveyed the next procedure they would like to try.

"Mrs Boland, there is a device called a cervical-ripening balloon catheter. It is a device that we insert into your cervix that will manually force your cervix open."

I felt sick. Not only was this the first time such a procedure had ever been mentioned to us, but the thought of this treatment on top of the pain I was already in was unfathomable. Perhaps it is one of those things that sounds far worse than it actually is, but I have to tell you, at that moment, it sounded like the most horrific thing in the world. There was no way. Not only did it sound tremendously painful, but it was also going to take many more hours.

I stopped the doctor in his tracks. "No."

He looked at me and was about to add to his argument, but I cut him short. "No."

I looked at my husband, and I knew I had his support. This was not going to happen. I had spent the past two days with unfamiliar doctors intermittently violating my personal space and causing me pain, and I had had enough. I could not entertain the idea of another internal examination. It was too much.

"Well, Mrs Boland," he said, "I can see you are in a very difficult place at the moment. Perhaps it is best if I give you some time to think it over. The only other alternative I can suggest is that I give you an internal examination and see if you have dilated enough to break your waters. That should help to bring on labour."

For the first time, I sensed something in a doctor that I had not sensed since Dr Hart. It was veiled, but it was there: compassion. This doctor felt some compassion for us. I could tell from how he had made his last remark that he was working for us, not against us. I believe he could see that breaking my waters would force something to happen, one way or another.

Then the doctor came and sat next to me and said the nicest thing a doctor had said to me throughout this entire ordeal. "I can see this has been a terribly difficult decision for you. I keep thinking about what I would do if my child had received the same diagnosis, and to be honest, I would have probably proceeded with the pregnancy also."

Wow. That was the first time a doctor had tried to relate to us. There was hope after all.

He continued putting forward his case about the balloon, but he could see that I still uneasy about having the internal, so he

The Arrival

again suggested he would return in an hour or so when I had had some time to rest.

Fine by me. There was no way that balloon thingy is going to happen—not now, not ever.

When he left the room, my husband cuddled me. He knew it was too much for me, and he supported me 100 per cent in refusing the treatment. My husband is a man who speaks his mind and tells me his truthful views on a situation, and I am so grateful for his honesty. I can trust what he says as the truth, so when he told me that he was in 100 per cent agreement, I knew he was not just giving in to the situation. He genuinely agreed. This was too much.

When the doctor returned, I had thought through the situation. If he was able to break my waters, this saga could not drag on longer. Even if I was not able to be induced, at least with my waters broken, they would *have* to do something—surely. It was already Thursday afternoon. I had been in hospital since Tuesday morning. Surely this was getting beyond the realm of the ridiculous, even for the medical staff.

So the doctor gave me the internal exam, and he ascertained that my waters could be broken, so I was sent upstairs in relatively short order to the birthing suite. Things were finally happening! I was wary and exhausted, but we were both excited. It would not be long now until we got to meet our little boy!

I had asked for an epidural because I knew I was at the end of my physical and emotional limits. When the anaesthetic had taken affect, they broke my waters and began administering the Syntocinon into my blood stream. (Syntocinon is a drug used to bring on contractions.) I could feel the tightening of my uterus begin, but as time wore on, the contractions became less severe and eventually stopped. Not to worry—there were still three more increments of Syntocinon they could administer. They upped the dose, and the contractions began again.

Another twenty minutes passed, and the contractions wore off again. Not a good sign. Time and time again they increased the dose of Syntocinon, and time and time again it wore off. Hours had passed, and nothing was happening. It was torture.

Finally, we were only one increment away from the maximum dosage they could administer. I had thought to myself, *This is it. They have no other alternative now. They will have to perform the caesarean section.*

Oh how wrong I could be! The doctor was called in to examine my situation, and once again we hit the wall. The caesarean section was not considered or agreed to.

This was *insane!* My husband and I looked at each other in disbelief. There was no explanation given, no alternate plan suggested. Clearly my labour was not progressing, and they had only one more dose of drugs they could give me. I was physically and mentally shattered. What the hell were they thinking?

Michael had had enough. My husband is usually a quiet man who does not like to create a fuss. Not now. He will be the first to admit that he is not the most eloquent of men. He sometimes struggles to express what he means. Furthermore, where medical terminology and procedures are involved, he has a level of fear that people will not take him seriously because his wording might not make sense.

But never before have I been more proud of my husband. He was forceful yet respectful. He struggled to find words to express himself, but he did it nonetheless. He stood his ground before the head of the department and told him that no resolution was completely unacceptable and action needed to be taken. He was not abusive. He was not malicious. He is my absolute hero and all the more because I knew how difficult it was for him to do.

To this day, I have no solid explanation for their behaviour. The doctors I have since spoken to also have no explanation. In fact, they are horrified it ever reached that point. It was truly irrational.

The Arrival

The only thing I can think of is a spiritual wall that was preventing the doctors from seeing reason or having compassion. The doctor who had shown me compassion earlier had finished his shift, and this doctor was unmoved.

Now, among all of these goings on, there was another saga playing out. On the home front, my mum and dad had been looking after our children. They had fully expected (as we had) that our baby would be born either Tuesday or Wednesday of that week, and it was now Thursday night. Some weeks before we had known Stephen would need to be induced early, my mother had made a commitment to teach a workshop all weekend in another city—a city about 1,000 km from where we were. In the midst of our fighting doctors and frustration, Michael received the call from my parents letting us know that they were both planning to honour their commitment in Melbourne in spite of the circumstances.

At the time, I was too far caught up in my own world of pain to really have this news sink in. In fact, it was not until many months after Stephen's birth that I realized the gravity of this situation. Here I was in the worst moments of my life. I was bringing my parents' grandchild into the world, and the window of opportunity for them to meet their grandson was likely to be so very small. How could they possibly choose to drive 1,000 km in the other direction? I will regret the decision they made for my entire life, but I was in no position at the time to do anything about it.

So there we were, alone in the birthing suite. Doctors were not listening, and my parents had abandoned us. The more pressing matter was to have something done about this labour, so we did the only thing we could do. We prayed. We prayed that God would remove this wall—this block that was preventing the doctors from seeing reason. When we had finished praying, our midwife came into our room. She could see I had been crying and asked what the problem was. We explained the situation as best we could, and she was grieved for us. She offered to go and speak to the doctors on our behalf. It was our best shot.

I am brought to tears when I am reminded of how God answered our prayers. Not more than ten minutes after we had prayed, there was a change of shift in doctors. New faces, new minds. The wall had been brought down, and with a little discussion, the new doctor agreed to the caesarean section as the course of action. Hallelujah!

I was put on the immediate waiting list for surgery even though it was late at night. As it happened, there were two emergency procedures that needed to happen before me, but I didn't care. Our baby was going to be born. As we waited, one of the doctors brought in his personal mobile phone. Someone on the other line wanted to speak to me. I held the phone to my ear, and I heard the voice of our overseeing obstetrician at the hospital—the one who had given us so much resistance to start with.

"Hannah," he began, "I have had a talk to the other doctors, and we have agreed that the caesarean section is now the way to move forward. In a way, it was a shame that they broke your waters. Otherwise you could have gone home for the weekend and we could have tried again next week, but I suppose it's too late now."

It took every fibre of my being not to throw the phone across the birthing suite. This doctor simply had no clue. He had no understanding or desire to understand the position we were in. Even at this stage of the game, he would have let it carry on for days. What an abomination.

Thankfully, though, he was not there to interfere with proceedings, and finally, after more than sixty hours of painful and mentally torturous treatment, our beautiful son, Stephen Michael Boland, was born at 11:32 p.m. by caesarean section, weighing 2.97 kg and measuring 50cm long.

The Arrival

In spite of the circumstances and the agony of the days just gone, it was one of the most beautiful moments of my life. To hear him cry for the first time was absolute joy. He stunned the theatre staff with his loud, healthy cry. It was a far cry from the gurgling, dying child they had expected to see. He was healthy. He was pink. His face was beautiful. He was perfect. I watched the tears streaming down my husband's face as he held his precious son in his arms for the first time. Stephen was here. Praise the Lord!

8

A Servant's Heart

I enjoyed cuddling my son. When I was finally able to sit up after the surgery had finished, I held him for the first time. It was surreal. Here he was, my beautiful, pink baby. But even in those first moments, it was difficult. Stephen was struggling to breathe. He kept gasping in little breaths. He seemed to be breathing okay, but it was a struggle. He was fighting for more air.

The nursing staff made a special allowance for us under the circumstances. Since we had no idea if Stephen was going to live for minutes or longer, they allowed me to carry him into the recovery ward, and Michael was able to sit with us. It was a precious time. It was the first time the three of us had been left alone together since he had been born only about twenty minutes earlier. As we were left, Michael leaned over and prayed over our son. We were both so pleased to meet him and grateful for God's abundant blessing.

As I lay there, exhausted from the preceding days and recovering from major surgery, I thought I was ready to let Stephen go. He was struggling to breathe. I thought I had been so blessed just to be able to meet him. I said to Michael that I thought we should pray again and ask the Lord to take him quickly so he wouldn't suffer. Unlike my history of selfish prayers, I believe this was a genuine prayer to spare my son the suffering. I thought I was ready to let him go, so we prayed that the Lord would take him soon and that he would not suffer much.

When I opened my eyes, I wasn't sure what to expect. I think I was expecting the Lord to take him then and there because we had asked it with such genuine hearts. Once again, I am so glad in hindsight that the Lord's answer was no, not yet.

It was not long before I returned to my room on the ward. It was well past midnight, and both Michael and I were exhausted. The epidural still had twelve or so hours to wear off before I could walk or even move around properly in my bed, so Michael took the first shift of child minding. Stephen was in his own crib, gasping for air. He had also become quite unsettled and was starting to whimper.

It was tough to listen to, both because it indicated my son's suffering and because it was preventing us from resting. Again, it was a selfish response but perhaps very understandable. I had not slept properly in three nights, and with the physical stress that had been placed on my body I desperately needed rest. In some bizarre way, the fact that I was already frustrated with my baby gave me comfort. Here was our baby, and I was already suffering the sleep deprivation and frustrations that come with a newborn. Yep, he was definitely part of the family.

I will never forget watching my husband lift Stephen out of the cot and putting him into the foldout bed with him. I will also never forget listening to Stephen start to settle down as he cuddled into his daddy and had a long rest. He began to stop fighting for breath and seemed more content, with a pattern of steady, shallow breathing. I am not sure how much rest Michael got that night, but he often reflects on that memory as one of his fondest with Stephen. I often reflect on this memory as one of my fondest of Michael.

I was very excited come morning. Stephen was doing well, and it looked as though we were going to be able to introduce him to his sister and brother. I called my sister and asked her to make the hour-long journey with my kids.

In the meantime, Stephen had become more unsettled. As with most newborn babies, I guessed he was hungry, especially since he had not yet had a feed. So in conjunction with the nursing staff, we agreed to insert a feeding tube through his nose and try a small amount of formula.

I was so nervous. For me, this was the make or break. Stephen was so healthy in every other regard. He was a strong, healthy boy for a baby born at thirty-four weeks. If he was able to accept feeding, I felt it was a good sign that he might live for a long time and we would be able to take him home.

I watched the nurses lift the little vial on the end of the tube, and the liquid slowly began to pour into Stephen's stomach. It was not long before my restless little boy was content, with a full belly. How my heart rejoiced! He was feeding! He was well! I was going to be able to bring him home and care for him!

It was not long before Allison and Harry arrived with my sister. They had been excited for weeks to meet their baby brother, even though they knew he was very sick. As they walked into the room, I was overwhelmed with joy that they were able to meet their brother. We had not known whether this would ever be able to happen. I was so grateful that God had not taken Stephen when we had asked him to.

It was the only time Allison and Harry got to spend with their brother. It was as short visit, filled with cuddles and questions. I still wasn't able to move from my bed, but I happily snapped away photos from where I lay as I watched my husband help our kids hold and kiss and cuddle their baby Stephen. My one regret from this time together was that we never had a photo taken with the five of us together, but this memory of my three children together is one that will not fade quickly. It was such a special and precious time—perhaps my best ever family memory.

We were still not sure how many hours we would have with Stephen, so we were eager for family to come and visit, and we were very pleased when Michael's parents arrived to meet their grandson.

Stephen had been moved into a special crib with a heated water mattress. He had been unsettled again, and we found that his body temperature was around 34°c, far too low. In an attempt to raise his temperature, we transferred him into this crib, and we had been told to try and keep him on the water bed to raise his body temperature.

In our frazzled and exhausted state, we were not thinking properly. The biggest regret I have from Stephen's life is that when Michael's parents came to visit, neither of us thought to ask them to hold their grandson, and they never asked. How I look back on that moment and berate myself for not thinking more clearly and denying my in-laws the only chance they would have to hold their grandson. In fact, it was the only chance Stephen had to be held by any of his grandparents, and I missed it. It is one of those moments in life you can never undo, never make up for, and I am so deeply sorry. I know that there will be a part of me that will regret this for as long as I live.

After a morning of visits, we were glad for a break. I was desperate for the anaesthetic to wear off. I had been so awkward in bed that I had not been able to hold Stephen properly or for any length of time. I finally got the go-ahead from the nursing staff to get up, and for the first time, I was able to sit in a chair and nurse my son properly. It was beautiful. It was time just to have time with Stephen and my husband, and we enjoyed the quiet afternoon together. We had decided against having more visitors for the day. Stephen had been doing so well that we felt sure that we would have many more days for him to meet other family.

Stephen gradually became restless again as the day wore on, and the nurses administered another feed by tube. As he calmed once again, I watched my husband sit there and hold him. These are some of the most precious memories I have. He was telling Stephen all about his family: his brother and sister, his grandparents, his aunties and uncles. But the most touching memory I have is listening to Michael tell Stephen all about Jesus. He sat there and whispered words of love and comfort to Stephen. He told Stephen that he was beautiful and precious because he was made by God and that we were so honoured to be his parents. He told Stephen that Jesus loved him and that he was going to get to meet Jesus soon. How my heart fills with warmth and tenderness as I remember these things.

As the day wore on, the reality of the situation began to hit home. I started to inwardly panic. Was I really up to this? Stephen's body temperature was not rising, and if he was left un-nursed, he was restless. He had to be fed by tube. He was struggling to breathe. I suddenly felt inadequate as a mother to a level I had never before experienced. How would I cope? How could I take him home and care for him? I was overwhelmed.

Amidst these feelings of anxiety, we received a visit from the paediatric team. They were making their rounds on the ward, and for the first time, I realised my son was in official palliative care. I had never thought of it that way. For me, there was every chance that Stephen was nowhere near death.

I was grateful for the time the staff took to discuss matters of feeding and care for Stephen with me. I explained to them I was terrified of taking him home and not being able to manage, and I was assured that we would not be discharged home until I felt that I was ready to cope. That was a huge relief to me.

Yet there was one thing that struck me as extremely odd. The doctor kept talking about administering morphine for pain relief. He made such a huge deal about how a very small dose of morphine could be given to Stephen if we thought he was suffering in any way, but it was a *very* small dose and could in no way harm him or end his life.

If this had just been a matter-of-fact statement, I suppose it would have passed by me unnoticed, but he made such a huge deal about it. He kept stressing the fact that it would only be a "very small dose" and in no way enough to cause death. I guess he wanted to cover his bases so that if Stephen passed away after a dose of morphine, I was fully aware it could not be attributed to the morphine. A part of me saw the irony in the situation. Only hours earlier, the doctors at the same hospital were willing to do virtually anything to bring on labour at the expense of Stephen's life, and now that he was here, they were taking so much care to ensure that it was not their actions that caused his life to end. What a farcical situation, and one that grieves me to my core.

The doctors left, and the hours rolled by. We held our son and rested, but as we settled down for the evening, things became unsettled. Stephen began vomiting quite violently. This was not a good sign. I mean, I know babies vomit, but this was different. He vomited repeatedly, and concerned, I asked for a paediatric nurse to attend us. When she arrived, she decided to check the contents of Stephen's stomach by drawing fluid back up the feeding tube. We were all startled to see a measurement of fluid equivalent to much of the two feeds he had received. It appeared as though Stephen was not digesting well—possibly at all.

The realisation of the situation struck me with a sickening blow. I didn't know what to do. The nurse left us to discuss the course of action, and I broke down in tears. The shocking option before us was to try feeding Stephen again in the hours to come or to cease feeding. This is a choice no parent should have to make.

And I couldn't. This was one decision that was beyond me, and I knew it. My tendency was towards not feeding him again, but I was so concerned that my motive for that was my fear of him living. I was so twisted and so utterly unfamiliar with the depths of my own heart, and I knew I could not make this decision.

There are many moments where I have pitied men in general and my husband in particular for being the head of the family. It can be a truly unbearable task, and I am often thankful I do not have such responsibility. Every part of me wanted to be able to help and support Michael as the ultimate decision maker in this moment, but every fibre of my being failed me. It broke my heart to have to put it all on him, but what more could I do? If I had suggested to him what I was inclined to suggest and he made his decision based on my inclination, how could I ever forgive myself if I later realised my motivation had been selfish? How could I ever expect him to forgive me?

So I told Michael that this was too much for me. He had to make the call, and I would support him in whatever he decided to do.

I was amazed at the strength my husband showed, and how I have admired him for it ever since. I had started to doubt my perception of the situation. I thought that perhaps the amount of fluid drawn from Stephen's stomach was not as much as we had thought; perhaps he was able to feed after all. But Michael was sure. He had seen it with his own eyes, and he knew the harsh reality. He made the call, and I love him for it. We were not going to continue feeding Stephen. He might only have hours of life left, and we were not going to subject him to hours of vomiting and suffering when it was highly likely he would not digest his food.

Many months after Stephen's birth, I was talking to a good friend of mine who is a paediatric nurse. We were talking about sick children and the tough decisions people sometimes have to make. She was remarking that in Stephen's case, she was sure that if I had a feeling deep down of any possibility that we might have been able to save Stephen's life, we would have done it. I'm not so sure. Once again, I was staggered by my own selfishness in a situation where my son's life hung in the balance. My main concern was how I would cope if he kept on living. As a result, I don't believe deep hardship and suffering always bring out the best in people. Often I think they can reveal the worst.

Even after the decision was made, I was uneasy. Stephen was unsettled, and we probably still had time to change our minds. But as the hours wore on, I accepted the fact that regardless of whether it was the right decision, it was the decision.

It was another sleep-deprived night. Stephen was unsettled, and Michael and I took it in shifts to cuddle and calm him. To keep his body temperature from falling, we had to undress Stephen and put his bare skin on our own bare chests and cover him with blankets. To do this safely, we had to be sitting upright in a chair. After almost two days straight of being flat on my back, the plastic hospital chairs were harsh. I regularly lost feeling in my bottom and my legs. Nevertheless, they were some of the most beautiful cuddles a person can experience. Stephen was nurtured on our chests, and he was quiet and sleeping peacefully. Each time we attempted to return him to his crib for some rest, he became unsettled.

Michael took the final night shift until the dawn, and I awoke to glorious sunshine pouring through the window. I had had some sleep, and the combination of refreshment and sunshine sent my heart soaring. It was going to be a good day. I felt for the first time that I could cope with what lay ahead.

Newborn babies can potentially last for many days without food, and Stephen was doing very well. I felt sure it would be a slow decline and that we would still have a number of days to enjoy his life.

I was still uneasy about our decision to not feed him and its implications. Even though the decision had been made, I felt like I needed to talk it through with someone. I needed a good friend—someone who knew me and understood me well. Michael had gone home to have a shower and spend some time with the children, and I asked him to contact my best friend to see if she could come and spend time with me.

There is nothing in this world quite like a godly friend. Clare is a woman who has walked with me ever since I became a Christian, and we have had the privilege of supporting and loving each other through some of the best and worst times of our lives. Clare had shared the months of struggles before Stephen's birth with me. She had prayed with me, supported me, and encouraged me. I am ever grateful to God for a friend like Clare.

As I placed Stephen into her arms, I watched the tears roll down her face. Clare's family and our family are very close, and I know that holding Stephen was in many ways like she was holding one of her own. She had shared the months of anticipation with me, and I felt a true pang of motherly pride as I was finally able to introduce her to my son.

The hours she spent with me that morning are some of the fondest we have spent in our friendship. I offloaded all the events of the week and all the tough decisions we had to make onto her, and she encouraged and supported me every moment.

She left because my sister and brother-in-law had come to meet Stephen, and for a moment I was surrounded by people who love me and care for me as deeply as any people can. How I am blessed by the godly love and support of these three people in my life.

Not long into my sister's visit, lunch arrived. I was famished. I had been running on empty in every sense of the word.

Perhaps this would be a good time in the story to detour for a moment. There is something many people (including myself, up to that point) don't really think about. If you have a loved one in hospital for an extended period, and that person's spouse is spending most of his or her time at the hospital with him or her under quite intensive circumstances, meals can be quite hard to come by. In many hospitals, meals are provided for the patient but not for the spouse. The nature of our situation meant that times we were able to eat fell outside of cafeteria hours, and vending machines only do so much. A practical way to be of use in this situation is to bring some mobile meals along with your visit or drop some off at the administration to be passed on. It will truly make a difference.

Michael and I had been splitting meals between the two of us, so I was ready to tuck into one of the few solo meals I'd had in over three days. My sister was more than happy to nurse Stephen for me as I ate my lunch. It was nice to have a sense of normality to the situation. There I was, a happy mum in the hospital, chatting with my sister and her husband and watching them cuddle my newborn son. This memory is so vivid in my mind because of what happened next.

When I finished my lunch, I went to take Stephen back from my sister, and my heart immediately sank. She hadn't noticed while she was watching him, but the difference in Stephen's complexion and demeanour had drastically changed since I had begun my lunch. Beforehand he was already starting to look dehydrated, and he had certainly been less pink than the day prior. Now he was a sickly grey colour, and his eyes were sinking back into his head.

I called the nursing staff immediately, panicked that something was going to happen while Michael was not there. Maybe I was overreacting, but my heart was sinking lower and lower. When the nurses arrived, they took one look at Stephen and suggested that he might be made more comfortable with some morphine. I hadn't even noticed until that moment that he had been in pain. I was immediately aware that every time I moved or changed position, he was actually groaning slightly. He *was* in pain.

The thought of morphine struck me like a lead weight. How had we gotten here so soon? Today was supposed to be a glorious day, and tomorrow he had more family to meet. This couldn't be.

Michael and I had already discussed the day beforehand that if either of us were left alone in a situation to make a decision regarding Stephen, we would do it and fully support the one who had made the decision. I could see from Stephen's face that the morphine was only going to help him. There was nothing else that could be done.

As the nurses fetched the medication, I rang Michael and told him he needed to return quickly. I was so worried that Stephen might pass away before he returned. I also told him to ring his sister and invite them to come quickly to meet Stephen. I had thought we would have all afternoon and evening for their visit, and now I was worried they might miss it altogether. Everyone was soon on their way.

I had always thought the term "broken heart" was a nice, poetic expression relating to an overall experience or feeling someone has when he or she is grieved. I have since changed my view. I can actually pinpoint the exact moment where my heart tore in two. When I listened to my baby cry as the nurse administered the injection, I knew it was the end. I didn't know how close we were, but I knew beyond a doubt that in the next few hours, we would face the awful task of watching our son die.

I sobbed with overwhelming sorrow. I watched my sister and brother-in-law stand by helplessly. I knew they were praying for us then and there, but they were otherwise so helpless. I was so helpless. All I could do was watch my baby boy fade away in my arms.

It did not take long for the morphine to take effect, and I was relieved to see Stephen settle and feel him relax in my arms. I asked for my sister to stay with me until Michael arrived. I did not want to be alone. It was perhaps the most intense and intimate moment my sister and I have ever shared, and I will always be grateful for her love and support, especially during those hours.

That time together meant even more to me in the absence of my parents. Mum and Dad never made it back in time to meet Stephen, so Stephen's life was only shared in my family with my sister and brother-in-law. Even before we knew of Stephen's complications, I had always enjoyed the thought of watching my father hold his grandson in his arms and pray a family blessing over him. I had enjoyed that thought even more since we had learned the news of Stephen's condition. How it still breaks my heart to think that opportunity was missed.

Michael's smiling face was soon at the door, and I breathed a huge sigh of relief. I knew he would be a little worried, but he had not yet seen Stephen. Our boy was a different boy from the happy, pink baby he had left behind that morning. As he walked over to me, the reality of the situation began to dawn on him.

Not long after my sister and husband left us, Michael's sister and husband arrived to meet Stephen. He was in such a bad way that I thought he might very well die during their visit. As my sister-in-law entered the room, she walked right over to me, put her hand to my face, and kissed me on the cheek. I watched the grief fill her face as it filled her heart when she looked down at her beautiful nephew. And then she whispered the six most beautiful words I have ever had spoken to me by a friend: "You guys have done so well."

How those words were music to my ears, music to my heart. Sadly, it was the first time anybody had said to us, "Well done." How my heart soared with such encouragement. They were words I needed to hear.

I wanted her to be able to hold Stephen, but I found that I just could not hand him over. I felt that he could pass away at any moment, and the thought of him dying in someone else's arms was more than I could bear.

As it happened, it was only twenty minutes after they left when Stephen's breathing became shallow. We felt like something was about to happen. Michael was holding Stephen, and as he teetered on the brink of death, I listened to Michael pray over him. He thanked God for the privilege of being Stephen's father. He thanked God for the time we had with him. He asked God to look after Stephen, and he told Stephen that his race had finished.

Then it happened. Stephen stopped breathing. His face turned bright red, and his eyes rolled completely back into his head. After a moment of intense suffering, he was still. This was it.

Michael fell to pieces as he held our son. I hugged Michael around his neck and looked him in the eye to tell him how proud I was of him and the father he was. We spent a moment looking at the silent, still figure before us, and I went out to inform the nursing staff of what had just taken place. They would send down a paediatric nurse as soon as possible.

You can imagine our shock when, as we sat waiting for the nurse, Stephen suddenly began to gasp for breath. Michael was so startled that he almost threw Stephen into the roof. What was happening?

By the time the nurse arrived, Stephen was breathing regularly again, and Michael and I sat stunned. This wasn't right. We had said our good-byes. We had watched him die—or so we thought.

There was not much for the nurse to do. Enough time had passed since the last dose of morphine, and we agreed to another dose to ease his suffering. We were told that there might be many more hours of these false alarms ahead. As I watched them administer the injection, I realised that something was different. Stephen did not cry this time. His poor little body was so far beyond it that he could not even respond to the pain of the injection. Perhaps he didn't feel it.

It was a long night. We lost track of the number of times Stephen appeared to die and then moments later, sometimes even ten minutes later, he would begin to gasp for air. The physical and emotional stress of this experience is indescribable.

The nursing staff members were amazing. They kept checking in on us and giving us ideas on how to make Stephen more comfortable. Stephen's lips had become dry and cracked, so they gave us some swabs to help keep them moist. He also seemed to like a sugary fluid the nurse gave us, which we were able to drip onto his tongue.

Each time Stephen "died," and each time he started breathing again, he was less and less present with us. He grew weaker and weaker. Perhaps the third or fourth time this happened, I was at my breaking point. It was not supposed to be like this. We had said good-bye so many times, we had cried our hearts out, and still it went on.

When Stephen started breathing again, I said to Michael, "I can't do it anymore. Why can't he just die?"

That was the raw emotion of my soul, and even now I am ashamed to admit it. As if it was all about me! Here was my son dying, suffering, and once again all I could think about was how it was hard on me.

I have spoken of many moments in this story where my husband has blown me away, but there is none more than what he did next. He was as emotionally and physically undone as I was, yet he lovingly took Stephen out of my arms and he said, "Well, mate, you're still here for a reason. And as long as you are still here, I am going to serve you as best I can." He then reached for the cotton swab and began swabbing Stephen's lips with the gentle touch of a loving father.

I have never witnessed a servant's heart as I did that night. I have never felt so utterly ashamed as I did in that moment. Michael hadn't done it to shame me; he had done it to serve his son and set an example. Michael often remarks that he does not feel like he is a good leader, but now I remind him about his servant heart towards Stephen in those moments. I have never witnessed such an extraordinary, selfless, and tender example of leadership in my life. I immediately repented of my attitude and joined my husband in making Stephen as comfortable as we were able.

As with many highly anticipated events, it happened in a way we did not expect. After so many false alarms, Michael gently cradled Stephen in his arms while I checked my email. It was now well after ten o'clock at night, more than five hours after the first time Stephen had stopped breathing. It could have gone on all night.

As I scrolled through the loving messages of support sent by family and friends, I heard Michael whisper to me, "Hon, I think he's gone."

"Yeah, right!" I said, thinking it would only be a matter of time before he started breathing again.

"No really. He looks different this time. Come and see."

As I strolled over to where they sat, he was right. Something was different. Stephen's face was slightly yellow. This was new. But I wasn't convinced.

We called the nurse down, and as we waited, Michael asked me to take Stephen from him. He couldn't go through another false alarm. He wouldn't cope with a gasping Stephen in his arms.

It was a tense wait. There were no tears. There was no gasp either. The nurse finally arrived and checked for a heartbeat. She stayed there for a long time, listening. After many minutes, she removed the stethoscope from her ears and put her hand on my shoulder. "I'm sorry," she said.

It was all she needed to say.

Stephen had quietly passed away in the late hours of a Saturday evening, a mere forty-seven hours after his birth. I felt numb. We both cried and cried.

Stephen's race was finally over.

9

Keith Green—the Ministry Years Continue

It was a glorious morning. Sun and warmth poured through the window. I had not expected to wake and enjoy the light, yet God had sent gorgeous sunshine to boost my spirit on what could easily have been the darkest morning of my life.

Michael had left for home first thing to see the children. Before him was the truly heartbreaking task of telling them their baby brother had passed away.

Alone I sat, waiting for Michael to return to the hospital with the kids. I washed, dressed, and sat quietly in a chair, enjoying the brilliant morning sunlight.

I decided to treat myself. I needed a little joy on a morning like this. Since joining our current church only six months prior, there was a name that seemed to be frequently mentioned: Keith Green. I'd never heard of him, yet everyone seemed to know who he was and his music. Both of the ministers at our church are huge Keith Green fans. One has even named his daughter after Keith Green's daughter who was tragically killed in the same accident that claimed his life. Other friends from church had memories Keith Green songs, such as family sing-alongs on car trips as kids. How could I have grown up playing music in church for over fifteen years and not know who Keith Green was?

So this was the morning. I flipped open my notebook computer and did the one thing that all die-hard fans of any band abhors; I purchased the greatest hits collection online and began downloading it to my computer. I had to see what all the fuss was about.

As I waited for the first few songs to download, I returned to my chair. It was difficult for me to get a grasp on the situation. The days of emotional and physical agony had left me exhausted and mentally numb. As I tried to process the few emotions I could actually feel, I found myself being grateful for the time we had spent with Stephen and grateful that he was no longer suffering.

In this vein, I started to contemplate my relief that it was all over, but as I did, a dark feeling started to come over me. It was the unmistakeable feeling of guilt. Had we really done the right thing? Should we have tried to feed Stephen again? Had we really done everything we should have, or had I just gone along with that decision to make my life easier? It truly was a sinking feeling. The more I thought about it, the guiltier I felt.

As I sank deeper and deeper, I knew within myself that if I continued down this path of guilt and entertaining these thoughts, I would never be able to forgive myself. I knew that guilt like this would tear me apart as a person, and I could not live the rest of my life always wondering whether I had done the right thing.

So I did the only thing I could think to do. Then and there I handed it over to the Lord. "Lord," I prayed, "I cannot go down this path. I know it will destroy me. I need your help. Please minister your peace to me, and take this guilt away."

Moments after I prayed this, I realised that enough of my new Keith Green songs had downloaded to start listening to them. I cranked the volume as loud as I dared, and the first few bars of "You Put This Love in My Heart" hit me like a freight train (but in a good way). He had not yet sung a word, but there was so much joy just in his music!

Over the next forty or so minutes, not only was I treated to so many beautiful and uplifting melodies and lyrics, but the Lord also ministered peace to my soul. With each passing song, I felt the guilt in me dissolve and the peace of God cover me like a warm blanket. Every single song had lyrics in it that God used to comfort me and to remind me of his goodness. Knowing what I now know about Keith Green and his relationship with God, it does not surprise me at all that God was able to use his music to minister such deep peace within me.

As I sat and allowed God's peace to cover me, I felt reassurance from God. I felt him minister his truth within me, and his truth was this: "My grace is sufficient for you" (2 Cor 12:9). I realised as I sat there that I could not vouch for every decision I had made on our journey with Stephen, but there was one thing I knew without a doubt: I had sought the Lord with my whole heart and relied on him for every decision and every outcome. Even though I may not have done everything perfectly, he was pleased with me because my heart had trusted in him. Yes, I had actually done something pleasing in the eyes of the Lord! Oh, for his glorious grace!

As if it wasn't enough to feel this conviction within my spirit, God truly blessed me that morning with his assurance. As the final song ticked over on the album, I found myself listening intently to the words and was blown away by what I heard: "Just keep doing your best and pray that it's blessed, and Jesus takes care of the rest..."[xviii]

Anyone who reads these lyrics without hearing the song could easily think this is a happy-go-lucky sentiment that takes a light-hearted view of our responsibilities in Christ. It is far from it. Times are tough, and we often do have a tremendous load of responsibility to bear, but the glory of Christ (as Mr Green points out in this song) is that there is only so much we can do. We have the responsibility to do our best, and our best is often hard work. But if we are wholehearted and humble, and if we truly seek the Lord in what we do, that is actually all we can do. Jesus really does look after everything else, including all those things that we can't do well in spite of our best efforts!

The Lord's ministry to my soul allowed me to greet Michael and my children with genuine joy and peace. They brought in a lunch of chicken nuggets and chips, and we sat and shared a meal together as a family for the first time in over a week. The kids had many questions about what had happened, and Michael and I did our best to explain. Only two days earlier they had sat in the very same room and cuddled their newborn baby brother, and now he was gone.

We talked and agreed it would be a nice idea to throw Stephen a special birthday party. Of course the best way to throw a great kid's party is to ask a kid what to include. Balloons, cake, and presents seemed to be the main ideas. As they left, I flipped open my notebook again and began to plan a birthday party for my son.

I freely admit that the party planning was a good distraction. In the days to follow, it kept me extremely busy. My days were filled with planning decorations, printing programs, organising gifts, and structuring the service. At night, I crashed in bed and slept soundly. The combination of party planning and recovery from surgery was the sleep stimulator I needed.

I revelled in planning this party for Stephen. I have always loved throwing parties and organising events, and I was determined to make Stephen's memorial service the best party I was capable of under the circumstances. In a strange way, I felt like it was helping me keep a very strong connection with my son. It was a way for me to honour my son and still do something for him, even though he was gone. I remember being filled with joy that week as I set about those tasks.

We tried to involve the kids in the planning as much as we could. The party was their gift to Stephen also. We curled ribbon for balloons. We tied blue bows around the necks of the teddy bears that would be our gift to each family—their very own

Stephen Bear to take home. We even baked a birthday cake with bright blue icing. By no means were we trying to pretend as though everything was okay and happy, but it was a helpful focus for our family for the week. It was also a practical way of reassuring our children that although we missed Stephen terribly, we were happy that he was now with Jesus. We wanted to remember and honour him and praise God for his life.

During those days of planning and busyness, Keith Green music was heard every day in our home. We chose songs such as "Create in Me a Clean Heart" and "Oh Lord, You're Beautiful" to feature throughout the celebration service. I am ever grateful for the music of Keith Green. As it turns out, I actually already knew many of his songs. His life and his music are enormously encouraging to me. It is awesome to think that even so many years after his death, God can still use his testimony and his gifts to reach out and minister peace and blessing to those who hear it. To this day, Keith Green music in our home is recognised as "Stephen's music" by our children, and I can think of no finer association for such beautiful ministry.

10

Great Expectations

I have always been a realist. Most of us picture the big events of our lives, such as weddings, special birthdays, graduations, reunions, etc., as being some sort of Hollywood film played out. We are so great at picturing things in our mind just how we would like them to be. The tricky part is whether we are prepared for the reality of what will be. Things are very rarely like the motion-picture equivalent of our minds. Accidents happen, children get sick, people make mistakes, freak storms happen, wedding dresses get stained before the wedding, and old men fall over. There is a wide variety of things that can spoil the "picture perfect" moment in our lives, but perhaps none as frequent as that factor known as expectation.

Expectations can be dangerous. If we have high expectations of an organisation, a friend, or a relative, sooner or later we are bound to be disappointed. If we have high expectations of how we expect to feel about a certain situation or how we would like an event to run, there is also plenty of room for disappointment. This is not to say that we should not have any expectations, but we should be very careful about the expectations we have.

Sadly, I had had many months to think about Stephen's funeral ahead of time. It was hard not to think about it. I had always known I wanted it to be a celebration of his life, however long it would be. In my mind, I pictured a church overflowing with family and friends, balloons as far as the eye could see, and voices raised to the heavens in song so strong it would send my spirit soaring.

The reality of the day was somewhat different. For us, the day was a mixture of joy, grief, and just plain hurt. In the morning, we worked for hours to blow up floating balloons to decorate the church hall. We set everything in place and organised gifts for all who attended. We then left the church and met our immediate family for a private burial service at the cemetery.

I don't know what my expectations of the burial were. Initially Michael and I had only wanted the two of us to be present at the burial because I dislike being around crowds of people, especially when I am so emotionally vulnerable. We were also reluctant to have Allison and Harry there because we could not think of how to explain that Stephen was inside the box when they were already beginning to understand that Stephen was in heaven. In the end, we decided to invite immediate family to the burial, and as the hour of the interment approached, we were still bereft of an explanation for Harry and Allison. Even on the way to the cemetery, I prayed and asked the Lord for wisdom.

After the burial, we were driving back to the church with the kids, and then it came; the big question. "Daddy, why was Stephen in the box?"

A light switch went on in my mind. No, it was more than that. It was one of those awesome moments when the Holy Spirit just gives you the answer, and the answer is so obvious you wonder why you didn't think of it yourself. In fact, it was *so* obvious I didn't know whether to be kicking myself for not coming up with it or simply rejoicing in God's answer to prayer. I decided to go with the latter.

"Well," I interjected, "Stephen's old body was sick, and that is the one that is in the box and is now in the ground. But God has given Stephen a new body—one that isn't sick—and that is the one he has now in heaven with God."

How awesome is our God?

I had high hopes for the rest of the service. There had been so much planning and so much preparation. We were ready to join in singing and praying with our families and friends to give thanks for Stephen's life. As we walked in to be seated, my heart sank a little. There were so many empty chairs. This was no one's fault in particular. It was one of those occasions where we put out too many chairs for the number of people to come, and even if the room is 80 per cent full, it still looks 50 per cent empty.

As I sat down and the service commenced, I had never felt so alone in my life. Yes, I had Michael and the kids with me, but the rest of my family members were all sitting in the row behind me, and Michael's family members were nowhere to be seen. There was a full row of empty chairs to either side of us. Mentally I knew that all of our family and friends were behind us, but it sure didn't feel that way. No one had even kept a program aside for us.

It was not that these things happened out of deliberate neglect; they were just things people did not think about on the day. Honestly, some of these things I never would have thought to do myself. However, I mention them so we can all learn from the experience and learn to be better friends and family to those who will need support in the future. We need to learn that on days such as those, we should go out of our way to look out for those who are suffering loss the most deeply. We should not just assume that everything is taken care of.

I must admit that my feeling of loneliness overshadowed my thoughts for most of the service. We sang songs and had a great address by our senior minister, but I don't really remember those things much. Sadly, my mind was focused on the empty seats and keeping my kids quiet. The music was not quite as overwhelming as I had thought it would be. I didn't have the feeling of being surrounded by love that I had imagined. I guess I was disappointed because I had a lot of expectations as to how things would be, and they weren't like that.

When it came time for Michael to stand and speak, I forced myself to concentrate. He hates public speaking. In spite of that, I was in such awe of the eulogy he had written of Stephen's life. There he was, in the deepest grief, and he was proclaiming his testimony of God's grace in his life to both his church family and his non-Christian family. It takes such guts to stand before those who have known you your whole life—those who think you are misguided in believing there is a God who cares for you—and proclaim the love of Jesus boldly, especially when your heart has broken. But he did it, and he did it awesomely. At that moment, I fell in love with my husband all over again.

After the service, I stood at the door and greeted everyone who had come to support us. It lifted my spirit. There were many more people there than I had realised, and we are ever grateful for the love and support of our friends and family who stood with us on that day.

Sadly, though, my expectations were not the only thing that cast a shadow over the difficult day. As we were enjoying fellowship and support with family and friends after the service, a family member who was deeply hurt not to be included in the private burial service during the morning publically confronted Michael. The family member also revealed to us that other family members who were not present at the service had deliberately boycotted Stephen's funeral because they too were so outraged by whom we chose and didn't choose to be a part of the private burial service.

How could this be happening? On the day we were burying our son, the family members who were supposed to be loving and supporting us were berating us because we had not handled things

Great Expectations

in the way they would have preferred. We had not met their expectations.

I have seen this sort of thing happen at weddings many times. I have always maintained that weddings seem to bring out both the best and the worst in people. Just ask anyone who has planned a wedding. Time and time again I hear horror stories of bridezillas or rude bridesmaids, lazy or unreliable grooms or groomsmen, over-demanding future mothers-in-law, disinterested fathers, and the list goes on. More often than not, the thing that seems to cause greatest offense at a wedding is when people have expectations, both realistic and unrealistic, and these expectations are not met.

I have heard of brothers who almost refused to attend a wedding because they were not chosen to be best man. I have heard of relatives deliberately giving stingy presents because they were so offended that their entire family of two hundred people was included in a function that costs more than $100 per head. I even knew a lady whose aunty made flower girl outfits for her children that matched the bridesmaids' dresses and kept pushing them into the official wedding photos even though they had not been asked to be flower girls.

People seem to place a lot of expectations on others. Do we really have the right to expect to be chosen as a best man or maid of honour? Do we really have a right to expect an invitation to a wedding? Do we really have a right to expect that invitations are worded in a particular way or that we will be giving a speech or that we should be included on every shopping and planning trip for the wedding?

I myself have fallen into this trap. Many years ago, two of my closest friends were getting married to each other, and I felt sure I was going to be asked to be a bridesmaid. I so desperately wanted to be a bridesmaid because I wanted to be there standing with them on their special day. They were a couple who had been many years in the making, through all sorts of highs and lows, and I had been there with them both through it all. You can imagine how I felt when I found out that I was not going to be asked. To make matters worse, my other best friend who was asked instead. It was truly a shock because she was someone I didn't deem to be particularly close to the couple.

I am still so ashamed of how I reacted. I was hurt. I tried to swallow it, but it churned in me for ages. My friend had known it would upset me too, so she had avoided telling me, which only made it worse. But as I stewed and stewed upon it, I began to realise how silly and selfish I was being. Just because she hadn't chosen me didn't mean that our friendship was any less valued. Obviously she had other friends in her life who were important to her that I wasn't aware of (I was living interstate at the time). She couldn't choose everyone for that position.

I came to realise that my expectation was an unfair one. Who was I to place expectations on the happy couple as they planned their event? They were freely entitled to make those choices without judgment or expectation. Yes, I had wanted to hold that special place, that title, and to be there standing at my friends' side as they took their vows, but I realised what an enormous honour it was even to be invited to their wedding. They still had enough respect and love for me to ask that I share and support them, even if I wasn't wearing the fancy dress.

In the end, Michael and I were so thrilled to be a part of their special day. Attending their wedding was one of the greatest honours of my life. I wasn't an official part of the service in any way. I was one of many guests there who love and cherish that couple, and it was a joy to be with them. I am so glad my own disappointment has not gotten in the way of our continued friendship, for these friends many years later made a twelve-hour return journey in a single day (with a twelve-month-old baby in tow) just to stand with us as we celebrated and mourned the life of our baby boy.

I am not saying that a bride and groom should not be sensitive and careful about how they plan their day and how they treat their families. Every family member and friend should be treated with respect and honour. But in the end, the marriage is about the two of them, and for the Christian, it is about them and God. It is important to allow those who love you to celebrate with you, but trying to meet all the expectations other people place upon you will only cause heartache and take you further and further away from what the celebration is about.

I am sorry to say that funerals have the tendency to be the same. Many people will grieve for and with those who have suffered loss, and if you are truly to love those who are suffering, seek to support them in the way they are asking for support rather than in the way you want to give it.

If you are ever supporting someone who has suffered enormous loss, I implore you to think about these things. Are you offended by what he or she has done? If so, why? Is it that your relationship is not as close as you thought it was? Do you feel dishonoured or disrespected? Have you been left out? Perhaps it is your expectation of the situation that is causing you more grief.

I am not suggesting there are not occasions when there has been genuine disrespect or bad behaviour. However, even in those cases, you still have a choice about how will you respond. Will you give an offended response or a response that only shows that person how much you love him or her? Overlooking an offense (genuine or not) is one of the greatest acts of love you can show a person. In fact, Proverbs 19:11 puts it this way: "Good sense makes one slow to anger, and it is his glory to overlook an offense."

In these times of deep grief, people simply need to be loved. In our case, the decisions we made about Stephen's funeral arrangements were never intended to cause offense or disrespect.

Ironically, we had taken other steps to ensure those very same family members were honoured during the service because we do love them and cherish them.

The painful truth is that my desire to forgive and move on from these events has been difficult. Mentally I have wanted to forgive and move on because I love my family and I know the Lord wants me to forgive also. But as I have begun to slowly move out my intense grief for Stephen, I have been astounded at how much the hurt from these things has cut so deeply—deeper than it would have cut under other circumstances. Perhaps it is because the wound from losing our son was already so profound. These events have caused additional hurt and upset that we have had to deal with, which is why I beg you not to put expectations on your loved ones who are hurting.

I am pleased to say there has been some reconciliation in our family over these matters, but sadly, there are still family members who are so offended that to this day have never acknowledged Stephen's death and refuse to speak to us. It has been an unnecessary shadow cast over the death of son, and one that is difficult not to recall when we reflect upon Stephen's celebration service.

However, we are grateful for the day of encouragement Stephen's service was to us. Friends and family from across three different states came to be with us. The ladies of our church put on an incredible afternoon tea and have loved us and supported us ever since. To this day, Allison and Harry remember our church as the place where we had Stephen's party. I am so grateful that we were able to throw our Stephen the only earthly birthday party he will ever know, and in my heart of hearts, I know I did everything to the best of my ability to honour him. That in itself is the greatest blessing I could have hoped for.

11

Friend with Benefits

I always knew it would be hard—I just didn't know it would be *that* hard. God was so faithful and gave us so much comfort and peace. Surely the hardest part of the journey was behind us. All of the anticipation and great unknowns were behind us. All of the resistance and unhelpfulness from the medical community was no longer a factor. We had met our son, and now we had buried him. We missed him greatly, but surely this was the time of healing—right?

I'm sure my friends thought I'd lost all grip on reality when I said things of this nature to them, and they were right. They could see what I couldn't. It was going to get a lot worse before it got better, but I was not ready for it.

You can imagine my absolute and utter shock when one week after Stephen's funeral, the wheels completely fell off the wagon. Emotionally, spiritually, and physically, I was in a black hole. I felt like the bottom had fallen out of my faith. It was the darkest place I have ever been—a true "dark night of the soul."

I remember being at home and feeling like God had utterly left me. This was more than just grief. This was abandonment. I was totally black inside, like a moving shell. I was completely lost.

And where was God? Why had he been so faithful, so gracious throughout all those months, and then when I really needed him the most, I had lost his presence and his comfort in my life?

Why, God, *why*? You are the God of comfort! You are the God who gives only good gifts to your children! How could you *possibly* leave me at a time like this? I have trusted you and given thanks to you for my son, and I have meant it! I have been faithful to your Word, I have obeyed your law, and I have not given into doctors who wanted to terminate Stephen's life and harm him. We have been faithful and have loved and trusted you. How could you do this to me! Where are you!

I have no words to adequately describe my feeling of absolute despair and total separation from God. When it came upon me, it lasted for a full week.

You may think, *A full week huh? That's not too bad.* But I tell you, when I was in the pit of grief and the Lord I love and who had comforted me was nowhere to be seen or heard, it was a week of sheer hell—and I don't use that expression lightly. For me, it was a glimpse into what eternity without Christ might feel like, and it was utterly awful.

So here I was in this pit of despair. I couldn't think straight. I was totally torn apart. Yet, even in my deepest despair, even in my darkest of dark places, I knew in the very pit of my being that Jesus is Lord, and my salvation was sure. I knew it. I couldn't deny it, but the suffering was so great that I found no joy in it whatsoever. That is the awful truth.

Day after day I read my Bible and cried out to God in prayer, "Lord, where are you? Why don't you answer me?" And day after day I received no reply, which only made it worse. I kept praying, "Lord, increase my faith. I know you have not forsaken me. Let me feel that you have not forsaken me."

Still nothing. Nothing at all.

Then one day, as I was sitting in my lounge, I was reading my Bible and crying out to God. As I sat, I heard the Lord say to me,

"Hannah, you know all of those things that you think you know about me? You know nothing!" Then he asked me, "What is the one thing you do know about me, in the pit of your despair, for absolute certain?"

I was freaked out—but not because I was hearing God talk to me (this was not a new experience). I was freaked out because in that moment, I had to face the fact that the only thing I was sure of—the one and only thing I knew about God from the core of my being—was that Jesus Christ was sent by God for my salvation.

So I confessed it to God, and as soon as I made that confession, the fog started to lift. I felt it physically start to lift. It was not a big clearing, but it was just enough.

It was not my confession of Christ as Saviour that caused God to lift the fog, because I have been a Christian for many years and have confessed Jesus Christ with my heart and my mouth daily. It was my admission that I in fact did not know God as I thought I did.

As I look back, I think I believed that my strong faith and trust in the Lord in the months leading up to Stephen's birth gave me the right to think that I somehow had a superior knowledge of God—you know, something to really show people. What foolish, arrogant pride! It was not until I confessed that God is too big, too high for me to grasp that I was able to begin healing.

It was a tremendous experience, but it was not long before I realised the desperateness of my situation. Yes, the fog had started to lift, but I was still in the thick of it. Furthermore, my faith was truly shaken. Everything I thought I knew about God was called into question, and as I prayed to God day in and day out, begging him to speak to me or show me something miraculous to prove he was there, I got no response. There was just a whopping silence from the heavens to give me no answers, no comfort.

"Just keep busy," was all that stayed in my mind. I had to stay busy. If I stopped, the reality of what had happened might just sink in. So I threw myself head first into everything I could think of. Cross-stitch. Gardening. Church. Play-group. Anything to stop me from thinking about my loss.

Deep down, I knew it could not last forever. Sooner or later, I knew I would physically collapse. But I didn't know what else to do.

I wept every day. I wept because I missed my son. I wept because I felt God had abandoned me. I wept because everything I had based my life upon, my faith in God, and my love for Jesus seemed completely unjustified, and it made a mockery of my life. I was a hypocrite. I had spent every day of my Christian life trying to show others the glory of God and tell them about Jesus. My whole approach to being a wife, mother, daughter, and friend was based on God's Word. I doubted myself in every action and in every thought. It was exhausting and soul-destroying.

So I kept blindly ploughing forward. I didn't know what else to do. My husband didn't know how to help me, and God apparently didn't want to help me. Things got worse instead of better, so one day, I bit the bullet and decided to see the doctor. Surely this wasn't normal. It had been three months since Stephen had died. Surely my grief should be dissipating, not increasing.

It is hard to explain being in this space. Mentally, I knew there was a God, and I knew Jesus to be true. Time and time again I have had testimonies to him and his works in my life—things I could not deny. But I was so emotionally shattered that it was impossible for me to feel anything. More than that, I knew my faith had left me. I had a head faith of sorts, but that deep conviction of the Holy Spirit had gone. It was a literal nightmare. Living day in and day out with that sort of inner conflict is horrific.

An interesting prospect was before me. How the heck was I going to explain all of this to my doctor? I was grieving for the loss of my son to be sure, but the thing that grieved me the most was

Friend with Benefits

the loss of my faith and the loss of God's presence in my life. My doctor was going to laugh at me and think I was a nut job.

As I walked into his consulting room, I found myself strangely at ease. He was a new doctor to the practise, and I had seen him only a few times when I had accompanied my parents to appointments. He was one of those people you instantly like. He had a gentle nature, he was thorough in his treatment, and he genuinely took an interest in what his patients were trying to tell him. As I sat there and tried to explain why I was struggling so much, it came as no real surprise to me to find out he himself was a Christian. He totally understood everything I tried to explain, and he gave me such encouragement. It was tremendous!

I remember bawling my eyes out in the car on the way home. Not only did my GP turn out to be a godly Christian man, but he had also been able to refer me to a Christian psychologist who had been recommended to me by someone in our church. Despite my lack of faith, I somehow knew that God was caring for me. It was almost as if he was saying to me, "Fear not, my child! I have my people looking out for you."

I approached my first psychologist appointment with some reservations. The fact that this woman was a part of our church (although I had never met her before) and claimed to be a Christian was a good start. However, I have had a lot of experience with people who claim to be Christians who are really nowhere with God. The last thing I needed was a so-called Christian without any depth of relationship with God. I had already made up my mind to not return for a second appointment if she said something as ridiculous as, "You just need to have more faith."

As it turned out (and to my delight), Lynda is a great, godly woman. She was swiftly able to diagnose me with posttraumatic stress disorder (PTSD), and we began months of treatment.

It is funny to consider my time with Lynda as treatment. I think it took more than two months of treatment just to bring

Lynda up to speed with the events of the past twelve months. Week in and week out, she would sit and listen to my story. She was shocked and horrified at the doctors' treatment of me during my pregnancy. She cried when I told her that my mother and father had never met Stephen because they had chosen to be Melbourne instead of with me.

Even more astoundingly, as I listened to the advice and direction Lynda would suggest during each session, I learned that of all the psychologists in the world I could have been referred to, Lynda was one who had been where I was emotionally and spiritually. She could relate to my faith struggles in a real way because she had been through it herself. Once again I felt God say to me, "Fear not, my child! I have my people looking out for you."

In truth, Lynda has never given me spiritual counselling. Her role as psychologist has been upheld and respected, even though she continually encouraged and enriched me spiritually. More so, I know that she prayed for me, even though she has never mentioned that she has. As the weeks rolled on, I found myself slowly starting to get a better grip on my own mind and my emotions. The grief and hurt were still very present, but I was beginning to cope better and sort through some of the rubbish.

When I returned to my GP a month or so later, we had a great discussion. He remarked upon the usefulness of a godly psychologist, and I was surprised to learn that the word psychology itself comes from the Greek word *psyche,* which means soul. It is literally the study of the soul.

I laughed as he related how many Christians believe that psychology is a lot of mumbo-jumbo and not necessary when we have God as our "Great Psychologist." Six weeks earlier I would have agreed with that point of view, but as I was learning, our human emotions are such a powerful factor in our lives that asking God to help fix our emotions can be like asking God to heal our sicknesses. Sometimes he absolutely does, but sometimes he does not. In those times when he does not, we need to learn to manage our illness, or in this case, our emotions.

As I write this book, I am still receiving treatment for PTSD. It is a long and difficult journey, and I am glad to share it with a woman such as Lynda. Professionally, there are restrictions on the social interaction between psychologists and their patients, but it has been impossible for Lynda and me not to form a deep respect and friendship for each other during our time together. We look forward to the day when my treatment is so far in the past that we can "officially" be friends. But as I laughingly remarked to her one day after a session, for the time being, she will just have to be my friend with benefits.

12

A Year of Firsts

For those of you who have had kids, you know how exciting that first year of their little lives is. Yes, there is also much angst and frustration in learning how to care for your newborn with a minefield of issues that need to be navigated: feeding, sleeping, bathing, teething, sickness, weight gain, weight loss, health complications—the list goes on. Add to that the long-term sleep deprivation (which has been used for centuries by organisations as a form of torture), and it is a melting pot for potential disaster.

Yet the year of firsts is also a year full of joy and excitement. There is the first time you get to watch the grandparents lovingly cuddle their precious "jewels" in their arms. There is the first nappy to change, the first bath to give.

Then there is the first trip to the shops. This is something that has consistently amused me. You can always spot first-time mums on their inaugural visit to the shopping mall after baby has been born. There are two key ways to spot them. They are the ones who are struggling with either an overloaded nappy bag to make sure they didn't leave the house without *anything* they might possibly need, or (and this is the clincher) they are the ones who are struggling in the car park to collapse the stroller into the car. Even copious amounts of practice at home making sure you know how to collapse the stroller (setting it up always seems so easy)

A Year of Firsts

cannot save the first-time mum from this fate. I know. I've been there. I've also seen it happen to others.

As time goes on, there are even more firsts. The first smile. The first words. The first steps. The first Mother's Day, Father's Day, and Christmas. And then there's the pinnacle of all baby's firsts—the first birthday. I have seen and been privileged to be involved in a broad spectrum of first-birthday parties. They have ranged from all-out mega-parties where large families and friends from all walks of life come and celebrate to relaxed and informal afternoon teas with immediate family and some excited grandparents. (I opted for this alternative with Allison, especially since my second child had been born only five days earlier.)

For anybody who has suffered the loss of a close family member or friend, you will know what a year of firsts can be like in another sense. Even those of us who are not by nature sentimental can be overcome with a sense of loss during that first birthday, first Christmas, first Mother's Day or Father's Day without your loved one.

After Stephen's celebration service, I had an excess of printed programs. These programs contained a few photos of Stephen and our family. It also had the order of service, song lyrics from our chosen choruses, and the beautiful "Father's Love Letter,"[xix] which is a collection of Scripture verses put together in such a way that it reads like a letter from God. I knew there would be people I would bump into around town who would see that I was no longer pregnant and would inevitably ask me about the baby, so I always kept a small stash of programs in my bag to hand to anyone who asked me about Stephen.

The first time I handed out a program was at my local supermarket. In recent years, I have spent some time building relationships with several of the staff at the checkout, and one lady had noticed I had had my baby. In a busy supermarket with people waiting in line behind me, I hastened to delve into my bag and pull out a program. As I tried to explain that he'd passed away, I was shocked at how quickly my emotions came to the surface. I had thought I was ready to tell people how proud I was of my son, but I wasn't. Seeing the shock and sadness in the checkout girl's eyes only added to my sorrow, and I quickly handed her the program and high-tailed it out of there before I became a blubbering mess in front of the rest of the customers. My coping skills had been serving me well while I was in my own home, surrounded by people who already knew the story. But this was the outside world, and I was not ready for it.

Several months after Stephen was born, we took our first family holiday in over a year. We went to Melbourne—my home city. It was a trip we had been planning since the start of the year. We usually take an annual trip to Melbourne to catch up with family and friends, and when we were first expecting Stephen, we had been looking forward to taking him on a family holiday and introducing him to our loved ones. When we learned of Stephen's complications, we had put off our trip until we were able to do so.

October came around quickly, and after the stress of the past few months, we decided it would be a great time to take that holiday and have some time together as a family. I come from a very small family. I have only one aunty and no first cousins, so we are very close to my aunt. My aunt, not having had children of her own, is almost like a fifth grandparent to our and my sister's children. Her house is stylishly covered with photos of the "grandchildren" and always has been. Therefore, it was no surprise to me when we arrived at her house that Stephen's photos were already printed, framed, and hanging on the wall. In fact, Stephen had won a place in a large photo frame sitting proudly in the entrance hall for all to see—a privilege that has not been afforded to any other "grandchild." My aunt hastened to tell us that those photos had not just been put up for the benefit of our visit, and I can honestly say the thought had never crossed my mind.

It was lovely to see our precious boy taking pride of place in someone else's home, yet every time I walked down that hallway on our holiday, I was torn. It warmed my heart to see my little boy, but each time I was reminded of him, I also found the hole in my heart grew a little bigger. This was a family holiday, yet all of our family was not with us. This was the trip where we were to be introducing our little boy to our family and friends. Someone was missing, and it seemed as though the more fun we had on our holiday as a family, the greater the pain of our loss became.

I am so pleased that my aunt had those photos of Stephen in her house. It was an acknowledgment of his life, and her comments to us about those photos were also an acknowledgment of our loss. It was actually the first time we had encountered such acknowledgment in our families (another first).

Now I am the first to admit that I am an intensely private person. I have always been this way. All my life it has been difficult for me to make myself vulnerable by sharing my innermost thoughts with my family and friends. My family, more than anyone, knows this about me.

I also know that I am quite a confident person, which people can mistake for being uninterested in the points of view of others. Perhaps you know someone like this. Perhaps it is a friend or even a family member. If so, I want to let you in on a little secret. Even those of us who find it difficult to express our emotions, those of us who have clear objectives and points of view, those of us who appear to have it all together—we feel a sense of loss and grief just as much as the next person. In fact, on some level, it makes it even more difficult for us to deal with our grief and emotions because usually these things are kept in check.

All through my pregnancy and for the months that followed, I was very conscious of being my usual jovial self when I was out with friends and family, but as you know from the previous chapters, behind closed doors I was a blubbering mess. This was not intentional on my part. Logically, however, when we are out and about and distracted by the events of everyday life, it provides a good diversion from our troubles. However, when the dust would settle at the end of the day (usually when things slowed down around dinnertime at our house), the distractions were fewer, and I often found myself in a pool of tears throughout the evenings and sometimes into the early hours of the morning.

I'm not sure if it was my jovial air or my off-putting confidence, but a few weeks after Stephen's death, still no one in our family would mention anything about him unless we were to bring it up. We were back where we started—does anyone really care? Or had everybody just moved on with their lives while I was stuck in an emotional rut, experiencing a year of firsts without any understanding from those around us? Imagine how it felt on our first Father's Day only two months after we lost our little boy when not one single family member offered a word of comfort or acknowledgment to Michael of how difficult the day must have been for him.

That being said, there is also nothing quite like companionable silence. To dwell in the presence of another and enjoy his or her company is a strangely intimate experience. The unspoken acts of love between individuals are a powerful expression of our love. But the trouble comes when you are unsure of the love and affection of your quiet companion. Is the silence truly companionable, or is it because you don't relate? This is a good question to ask yourself the next time you find yourself having companionable silence with someone. Our acts of unspoken love are powerful, but they should never be used an excuse to not tell our loved ones how much we love them.

I used to work with a girl who had been living with her partner for more than seven years. In all that time, he had never said the words "I love you" to her. She insisted that she was okay with this because she knew deep down that he loved her, but he just had trouble saying the words because of his upbringing. It came as no great surprise to me when I learned several years later that she and her partner were no longer together. Actions do speak louder than words, but words are still immensely important.

I realise that this is an interesting juxtaposition of emotions. On one hand, I was attempting to "get over" my own feelings and emotions related to Stephen's death while at the same time being upset that our close family and friends had seemed to move on. There were one or two family members and friends who would make the effort to stay in touch with me and regularly ask me how I was coping, and I am ever grateful for the blessing of these saints. Interestingly, it was often the people who did not know me who were the most eager to show their love and concern. Countless people stopped me in the middle of the street or at functions—people I had never met before—telling me how sorry they were for my loss and that they were praying for me. This has encouraged me so much in so many ways. The people who knew me the least were the ones who were encouraging me the most!

On the other hand, perhaps it is our discomfort with difficult situations that stops us from extending a word of comfort or encouragement to those in pain. We witness it all the time. We live in a culture that is steadfastly losing the art of building deep and meaningful relationships. On a more shallow level, we are becoming more and more selfish—unwilling to put ourselves out for anyone. We couldn't stop to help that old lady cross the street because we would have been late for our appointment. We couldn't possibly pause to talk to the man sitting on the park bench alone because he might think we are strange. How often we fail to act because it makes us uncomfortable to do so. It makes us vulnerable and open to criticism. It puts us out.

We often don't say anything because we don't want to say the wrong thing. However, saying the wrong thing with a right heart can often be more encouraging than saying nothing at all. In the weeks prior to Stephen's birth, someone close to me who had never mentioned the baby situation began telling me about a lady she used to assist in a volunteer capacity who had given birth to a baby with a similar condition. She went on to explain how hard it was for the mother to cope with such a demanding baby and the immense difficulties and strain it put on the family.

In one context, this was rather discouraging. The last thing I needed to be reminded of was how hard life was going to be if Stephen was able to come home with us. However, I could see that our situation with Stephen was a difficult topic for this person to talk about. I realised the conversation came from her nervousness about not knowing what to say and her desire to relate to me with her own personal experience.

We do need to be careful and thoughtful about what we say and how we say it. However, we also must be thoughtful when receiving words of encouragement and comfort from others. We need to have understanding of the well-meant intentions behind them.

So what is my point in all of this? Is it to berate our friends and family for their lack of care and thoughtfulness? By no means! Our family and friends care for and love us deeply, and we a grateful for each of them. However, I have learned that in our relationships, there are often more times than we realise when we should express the love and concern we are feeling and not just assume that the other person knows.

This is a classic mistake we make when loved ones are dealing with grief. We say nothing. We do nothing. We don't want to upset them. But I want to encourage you to do the opposite. Doing nothing is the worst thing you can do! Of course, there is a time and place for such conversations, and there also is a level of appropriateness that should be exercised. Don't expect your friend to spill her guts in the middle of McDonalds when you catch her on the fly and ask, "How are you doing, *really?*" This is a wonderful encouragement, and it goes a long way to show your friend that you care. By all means, ask the question; just don't expect an in-depth or even accurate response.

I would often get asked how I was doing on the fly by friends who genuinely cared. Each time I remember thinking to myself, *Should I give the playground response or the real response?* Being a mother with young children is such a lonely place to be at the best of times. The children are almost always with you, so finishing a full sentence is an accomplishment on its own, let alone delving into the deepest hurts of your soul. It can be a very lonely time indeed, even when you are not suffering any great amount of grief, because you simply cannot convey your thoughts and feelings to the other person in the time (and appropriateness of location) that you have.

Causing your friend or loved one to cry because you have referred to his or her loss is far better than making no reference at all. You are not the one who is making your loved one upset; it is his or her loss. Being with your loved ones, allowing them to be upset, and showing your support only provide you with greater opportunities to show your love and support in a tangible way. Don't push, but don't shy away from the situation either.

For those of you who know someone who is dealing with a difficult pregnancy or infant loss specifically, there is a fantastic organisation called Bears of Hope that has a leaflet designed especially for family and friends of loved ones who are suffering from a loss. It is a great list of "dos and don'ts" if you will.[xx]

Not acknowledging the year of firsts after a loss is a mistake I have made myself. My closest friend lost her dad to cancer only a few years ago. During that first year especially, I did think of her and pray for her often. I thought of her at Father's Day and

Christmas time, yet I failed to acknowledge it to her. It was only after my own loss that I realised my failings as a friend and asked for her forgiveness. How blessed we are to have a God who does not forget us even when humans do—a God of comfort.

Don't make the same mistakes I have made. People will be bombarded and overwhelmed in the initial days and weeks following their loss with genuine outpourings of sympathy and comfort. However, they really need your continued support in the long haul that follows. Be a good friend and a supportive family member. Acknowledge the year of firsts. Mark the dates in your calendar. Send cards. Make the call. Organise a coffee date. Fewer people are doing it than you think.

13

Head Joy or Heart Joy?

The church was beautiful. I had been coming to the church at St Stephen's for almost a year, but this was the first time I had ever gone into the original stone building and sat inside. It is a relatively simple stone church as far as churches of its era go, and my sister and I sat admiring the stained-glass windows surrounding us. Many were new windows that were obviously replacements for breakages over the years, and we were admiring both the differences and similarities between the old and new windows.

As families started to fill the old wooden pews, I was conscious that my sister and I seemed rather irreverent with our whispering and occasional giggles. My sister and I have always been able to find something in almost any situation to have a giggle about. We both love God, we both love the church, and we are comfortable coming before God in his house being filled with joy, which sometimes includes giggling.

That day I felt a mixture of deep joy and sorrow, and I would be lying if I said that all of our fun and light-heartedness came from a place of joy. It was a way for us to cope with what was before us. We were about to join more than a dozen other families in a Christmas memorial service that had been organised by the funeral home that conducted Stephen's funeral. The funeral home was not a Christian organisation, but it recognised that families who had lost loved ones throughout the year would find this first

Christmas especially difficult. Just ask people who have lost a loved one. That first Christmas is not the same as other Christmases. Most other people in their lives will have moved on, but for the family and close friends of that absent soul, he or she is deeply missed, particularly at times of family celebration like Christmas.

Just getting to the service had been a struggle for me. I was truly torn. Part of me wanted to invite both my parents and Michael's parents to the service in recognition of the grandson they had lost, but I was still so deeply hurt by the occurrences on both sides of the family surrounding Stephen's death. I could not bear to have them with me during a time when I knew my grief would come to the surface once again—a place where I was truly vulnerable. I needed someone with me who I could trust.

Michael had committed himself to an interstate function many weeks earlier, and we decided it was more important for him to attend that function than the service. I was supposed to attend this function as well, but we also agreed that the service was more important for me to attend to help me deal with my grief and hurt. My sister was able to be with me on that day, and I was once again grateful for her support.

So there we sat. As the service drew closer to a start, my sister and I became quiet and had a moment to reflect on what was before us. I had been dreading this moment. I had been dreading Christmas. As a child, I had always looked forward to Christmas. I enjoyed that special feeling of fun and festivity that gradually wears off as an adult. Since we had children of our own, we had begun some new family traditions that gave me a new enjoyment of the Christmas season, yet on this Christmas, my joy was nowhere to be found. I was in the darkest of dark places. I was not in control of my mind or my emotions. I was totally lost. I was thankful for the gift of Jesus, but I was far from joyful. I was in a world of hurt, and I was desperately trying to make sure that world of hurt did not prevent my children or our families from enjoying the season.

Head Joy or Heart Joy?

Frank, one of the funeral directors, stood up and offered his greeting to us all. As he spoke, I felt like I was on the brink of a breaking dam. The dam was still holding, but there was a crack down the middle that was getting larger and larger as the pressure of the water built up behind it.

If there is one thing that has always been guaranteed to crack open the floodgates of emotions in my heart, it is great worship music. As the first song, "Amazing Grace," was announced, I barely had time to gather my thoughts before I was standing and singing the first line, "Amazing Grace, how sweet the sound! That saved a wretch like me!" Well, that was it. It was all over. The dam burst, and I could not utter another word. My entire tissue supply for the service was exhausted by the end of the first verse, and there were three more to go.

I wonder, have you ever really listened to the words of "Amazing Grace"? Most people I know, either in my generation or older, are quite familiar with the song, Christian or not. But do people have any idea what they are singing?

> Amazing grace, how sweet the sound!
> That saved a wretch like me!
> I once was lost but now am found
> Was blind, but now I see![xxi]

I have often wondered what non-Christians think they are singing about when they sing this verse. Do they really know what wretches they have been? If they don't, how can they possibly know what amazing grace is?

There have been a number of times in my life when God has given me insight into just how much of a wretch I am. There was a time not long after Harry was born when God filled me afresh with his spirit and I felt his presence around me in a way I had never felt before. As I was praying one day, God gave me a vision.

As I looked at my body, it was like I was looking at my flesh with a magnifying glass. As I looked more closely, I saw that my body was not just flesh; it was deeply intertwined with splinters right through every part of my being. It was as though the splinters made up my flesh. They were so profuse that my skin was like salt and pepper mixed together. The splinters were so fine, so numerous, and so deeply ingrained that I knew there was no way on earth they could ever be separated from my flesh. It was impossible. They were a part of me.

Then it struck me what the Lord was showing me. He was showing me that the splinters represented my sin—not the sin I had consciously committed during my life but rather my heritage; my sinful nature. He was showing me that even my genetic makeup is so riddled with sin and filth, and it is so deeply ingrained, that even if I were to be the most obedient and godly person in the world, I would still be filthy in God's eyes because of my sin. It was a hopeless situation. Nothing could separate me from it. It was horrendous.

Hold the phone. Did I say that nothing could separate me from it? You know, as soon as I thought that, it's almost like I felt God smiling at me. He had shown me how great he is. Is anything impossible for God? No! Not even the removal of sin from our flesh. I mean, I had some understanding before that Jesus' blood held forgiveness for our sins, but I had no idea just how sorry a state we are in because of our sin! We are so far gone, so wretched, and so ingrained with sin that we are totally helpless, yet by the grace of God, through the sacrifice of his Son Jesus, we are made clean!

In that moment of singing, the grace of God—this "Amazing Grace"—meant more to me than it ever had. You cannot know the depth of the Father's love and the power of his grace until you first understand just how wretched you are!

Head Joy or Heart Joy?

Here I was in the depth of my sorrow—the darkest place of my life—but in some strange way, I also had joy. It was not an emotional joy. My emotions were taking me through the darkest grief a person can know, but it was joy nonetheless. It was joy in the knowledge that Jesus is my Saviour.

As I sat and reflected on this during the service, I realised again that it was possible for my emotions and my knowledge to be light years apart. In our postmodern society that preaches the philosophy, "If it feels right, it is right," this is a massive shift in mind-set. As a Christian, I have always known there is a reason why they call it faith; it is unseen and sometimes unfelt, and oftentimes we have to go against the grain of what we feel. Yet this was different. This was more than just being ticked off at the guy in traffic who ran me off the road and knowing that I should be praying for him rather than cursing at him. This was a place where I knew Jesus died for me and I knew I was righteous before God. I knew it in my being. So why wasn't this joy making me dance and rejoice in the aisles?

At that moment, I had another moment of revelation. It was NT Wright who said, "Christmas is not a reminder that the world is really quite a nice place. It reminds us that the world is a shockingly bad old place… Christmas is God lighting a candle; and you don't light a candle in a room that's already full of sunlight."[xxii]

This makes so much sense to me now. As I was sitting there with my heart bleeding on the floor of the church before God and man, I realised for the first time how shallow my faith had been. Jesus did not come to set all things right immediately. He does not make everything bad just go away. When we claim the promises of God for joy, healing, and provision, it is not to make our lives wonderful and easy-going right now. That is to come. We sinned against God at the beginning of time, and because God is just and cannot deny himself, he punished us with a curse that brings pain and suffering on a level we were never designed to endure. It was never God's intention for us to suffer like this when he created us. Our God-given emotions were given so we could experience the love and joy of intimate relationship with God our Creator and each other, not so we could mourn the deaths of our own children. Was it any wonder I was struggling?

I have reflected on this experience a lot since that Christmas service. It has changed almost everything about my relationship with God. As Christians, we tend to pray a lot for health, healing, and provision for others and for ourselves. These are not bad things to pray for, and God himself tells us to pray for these things. However, these requests should not be the sum of our prayers. It is a naive faith that says, "Everything will be okay because I have faith in God, and God has it under control" under the pretext that it means, "Everything will be okay." Romans 8:28 says, "And we know that in all things God works for the good of those who love him, who have been called according to his purpose" (NIV), but claiming that promise does not guarantee God will fix all of the holes and hurts in our lives. In fact, I believe he means the opposite in this verse. I believe that more often than not, he does not throw a miraculous fix our way so he can draw us closer to himself and grow us.

I often find the pruning analogy helpful here. If a plant had a nervous system like ours, the pain it would feel when it was being pruned back would be almost unbearable. (If you cut off a leg or an arm, it's going to hurt, right?) But what happens? The plant grows bigger, stronger, and more fruitful.

As I reflect on the faith I had up to this point, it was not wholly this naive faith I am talking about. I did not feel that God was going to heal my son. I knew that sooner or later, Stephen would die. I knew it would cause me grief, and I knew I was at peace in the knowledge that when he left us, he would be safe with Jesus in heaven. All of these things I knew at the time beyond a shadow of a doubt.

Head Joy or Heart Joy?

When I look back, however, I realise that I had another expectation that was unrealistic. I expected that God's peace would bring me emotional joy in the depth of my suffering that would override the suffering I was experiencing. I expected that God would heal my emotional wounds quickly and I would be able to move on with my life, safe and happy in the knowledge that Stephen was in heaven with Jesus and we were blessed to have been his parents. I had no idea just how deeply the loss of my son would grieve me. I was God's child, and I knew my son was in his care, so why was I so distraught? Why wasn't that hope and knowledge enough to stop me from sinking into the depths of depression?

Everything will not be okay for me in this lifetime. I have a hole in my heart and a hole in my family that will be with me every single day until I am with Jesus in heaven. It will always cause me grief and pain as well as joy and delight. All is not right with me in the natural, but it is well with my soul. It is well with my soul because although the pain and suffering is immense, the Father's love for me is so much more. Even in the depths of my grief, the blackest hours of my life, there is hope in Jesus Christ.

14

Jesus—the Founder and Perfecter of Our Faith

After many months of treatment for PTSD, one thing was becoming clear. My emotions, my grief, and my hurt were all starting to heal. Unfortunately, as I was able to clear my mind and process these things, it only cleared the way for one devastating truth: my faith was still a complete shambles. I had had glimpses of God, but I had written them off as the futility of my own mind.

I was not hearing God's voice. Oh, how I cried out to him and sought him in those months, but all I could helplessly do was to wait on him. It was not that sort of faithful waiting on him that sounds very nice and holy; it was waiting on him because I had no other option.

It was true torment. My head and heart were still not of one accord. I had so many doubts, and my self-confidence was still in ruins. Everything I had believed—everything I had based my life upon—seemed unfounded. I was the woman who was so determined to let everyone know that Jesus was Lord, and there I was sitting in my own lounge room, praying and crying and having difficulty forcing the words, "Jesus is Lord" through my own two lips in the silence of a vacant house.

Jesus—the Founder and Perfecter of Our Faith

I had looked up every verse I could find that had to do with faith. The book of Hebrews was my constant companion. Hebrews 12:2 says that Jesus is the founder and perfecter of our faith. I kept praying and praying, convinced that my lack of faith was not my fault. If Jesus was the founder and perfecter of faith, it was up to him to restore it to me. I clung to these verses for dear life and waited. Daily I read my Bible and cried out to God. Daily I waited on him. It was exhausting and uncomfortable.

About six months after Stephen passed away, I received an email from the wife of the senior minister at our church. She was inviting me to speak at the first big women's event for the year. It was a Shrove Tuesday event, and they were expecting between seventy and one hundred ladies to attend. I instinctively wanted to say yes. I love public speaking, and I love being an encourager. But how could I possibly say yes? My faith was in tatters. God himself had told me I knew nothing about him. There was no way.

I didn't know what to do. Every emotion and thought told me that I could not be of encouragement to anyone in my current state, but something was stopping me from saying no.

Then I had a brilliant idea. I hadn't heard God's voice for many, many months, and that was what I was yearning to hear the most. Perhaps now I could twist his arm because I knew he would not want me speaking to those ladies if it was not ordained for me to do so, and surely he would have to give me a clear answer!

So I prayed, "Lord, is this something you want me to do? I don't know how I could possibly do it, but I also am not sure that you want me to say no. I need an answer. I need you to tell me clearly yes or no."

Guess what? No answer.

I sat quietly and waited. I listened. No answer.

The next day came, and I sat in my chair. I just sat there and closed my eyes. Sometimes in the past when I have prayed, I have found it helpful to visualise in my mind that as I am praying,

145

Jesus is sitting in the chair next to me and we are having a conversation. It helps to keep the conversation real so I do not just treat him as a go-to man.

I sat and said, "Lord, I want you to come and sit in this chair and to meet with me."

As soon as I prayed it, I felt him say, "Are you really ready for that?"

In that instant, I knew exactly what he meant. He meant, "Are you sure you are ready to have me, Lord of the universe, come and sit with you?"

Of course the answer was no! I was totally freaked out! I bawled my eyes out at the realisation of my unworthiness to have my Jesus come and meet with me, and by the time I had collected myself, it was too late. He had shown up.

We talked about a few things. I soon realised I had been asking the wrong questions, so I said to him, "Lord, I'm so weak at the moment. I feel like you are talking to me now, but I know I am going to doubt it as soon as I stop praying. What do I do?"

He gave me just one word: "Trust."

I thought, *Ha! Yeah, good one God! Just trust. No problem. It hasn't worked for me for the past six months, so of course it will start working now.*

Putting that out of my mind, I then thought, *Right! We're on a good roll here. I'm going to ask him about Shrove Tuesday.* So I asked him again.

"Lord, do you want me to speak at this event? If you do, please tell me what you want me to speak about."

You'll never guess what he said.

Nothing.

I went about my day, but as I did, I churned and churned inside. My faith was so frail I was convinced it was my own mind. But as I churned, I really came closer to the feeling that the Lord wanted me to speak to the ladies and that it was my weakness that was going to make it happen.

Well, like I said, I had serious doubts that this was God. I was so unsure. I was chewing it over with Michael that evening, and as I sat there talking, I remembered that Paul wrote a passage about boasting in his weakness. I thought, *Hey, I'll look that up and see what it says.*

What amazes me every time I think about this story is how blind I was. The passage that I was about to read was a passage I had read many times before. I had studied it. I had prayed it. I had even memorised part of it. In spite of all of those things, I had no idea what I was about to read.

> So to keep me from becoming conceited because of the surpassing greatness of the revelations, a thorn was given me in the flesh, a messenger of Satan to harass me, to keep me from becoming conceited. Three times I pleaded with the Lord about this, that it should leave me. But he said to me, "My grace is sufficient for you, for my power is made perfect in weakness." Therefore I will boast all the more gladly of my weaknesses, so that the power of Christ may rest upon me. For the sake of Christ, then, I am content with weaknesses, insults, hardships, persecutions, and calamities. For when I am weak, then I am strong (2 Cor. 12:7–10).

I almost fell off my chair when I read it. Michael just looked at me. In that moment, I felt God's spirit rush through me, and he restored my faith. It came rushing back into me like a warm north wind, and for the first time in six months, I had conviction in my spirit. Hallelujah!

More than that, he blessed me. He gave me something else I had not experienced in more than twelve months. He gave me joy—not just the head kind but the heart kind!

I was so overwhelmingly excited. I felt joy in the fact that I knew it was God working in me and through me, because I was totally broken and unable to achieve anything on my own. It had to be God. He wanted me to speak to those ladies and tell them how hopeless I am on my own so that if they were blessed at all by hearing me speak, they would know that it was only by the grace of God that they were blessed.

It was truly a spiritual light-bulb moment, and it brings me such joy even thinking about it. God had chosen to put an end to my suffering, and faithful to his Word, he had used that suffering to bless me, to produce good for me, and to draw me closer to himself. My relationship with God is now richer and deeper than before, even though I realise I have so much more to learn and so far to go. It's like they always say—the closer you get to God, the further away you realise you are.

All of my suffering had not been in vain. I still have so much emotional grief to work through and forgiveness to exercise, but the Lord is with me, walking with me and talking with me, and I am making progress on every front.

Epilogue

There are so many things I hope you are able to take away from my story. First and foremost, it is deepest my desire that you have been able to share this journey with me and that in some sense, you have been able to experience the highs and the lows, as well as the immense suffering, so you also might be able to share in my joy at the grace of God.

Time and time again God has shown me and my family grace throughout this time of trial. He has shown me grace when I was unable to pray and converse with him as my grief and uncertainty overtook every other thought and facet of my life. He has shown me grace by allowing Stephen to be born alive and permitting us to share forty-seven of the most precious hours together. He has shown us grace in the decisions we have made, for better or worse, and he has honoured the intention of our hearts. He has shown me grace in the months of suffering and blackest of nights, for he has not let me out of his hand in spite of my faithlessness. And he continues to show me grace daily and hourly, for he wants to use me in spite of my wretchedness to do the most important work a person could do: to proclaim the gospel of Christ. Yes, this story is first and foremost about grace.

It is also my desire that you would consider more closely than perhaps you may have before the values our culture places on the deeper issues of life. It is so easy for us to fall into the trap of never giving socially accepted practices a second thought. But God tells us, "Do not be conformed to this world, but be transformed by the renewal of your mind, that by testing you may discern what is the will of God, what is good and acceptable and perfect" (Rom. 12:2).

Our culture is one that encourages us to put ourselves first: our comfort, our financial security, and our happiness. We are bombarded at almost every moment of our lives to pander to our own desires. Advertising is relentless: buy this outfit, drive this car, eat this food, invest here, start this project, improve your home—the list goes on. We are enticed every step of the way to feel happy, healthy, and wealthy, as though they are the best things we can expect out of life. I would much rather be suffering, sickly, and poor yet surrounded by the love of God and his saints than healthy, wealthy, and care-free but honouring myself as God and never knowing the true meaning of sacrificial love. We need to be discerning between blessings and grace or self-love and comfort. So often we deliberately ignore the true stumbling blocks in our lives because we have convinced ourselves those things are a blessing. They are no longer a blessing to us if they are drawing us away from God.

It is difficult to be holy and righteous in a world that is complex and grey. Even on the issue of pregnancy termination, I would not be so rash as to declare that there is never a legitimate or unselfish reason to terminate a pregnancy. There are so many variables and complications, and sometimes there are other lives at stake. These decisions are incredibly difficult and heartbreaking regardless of the outcome.

It is not about legalism. Jesus came to destroy legalism. He came to reveal the state of the heart. It is about our motivation. What drives our actions? Is it selfishness, comfort, laziness, or love? As I have experienced and shared with you, sometimes we are so emotionally distraught and inept that it is practically impossible for us to discern this for ourselves. At these times, all we can do is seek

Epilogue

the Lord and ask him to guide our footsteps. We need to cling to what is good and right and rely on him. It is His power that is made perfect in our weakness (see 2 Cor. 12:19).

It has also been my aim to give you insight into what people may be going through emotionally and mentally when faced with impossible situations, especially those suffering deep grief. In many ways it is one of those things you can never really understand unless you have experienced that loss for yourself. As friends and family members to those who are suffering, I hope that my experience has helped you understand what is helpful and unhelpful in your role as supporter.

Of course, not everyone is the same. Some people may need support in ways I have not outlined here. But here is the key: make yourself available on their terms, not yours. It is true sacrifice, and because it is sacrificial, it is the most magnificent kind of love you can give them. Make sure they know you are there waiting to serve them in any way you can. Make sure they know that you love them and are thinking of them. Be aware that your physical presence may be too much. If that is the case, you can show them you are present through cards, emails, texts, phone messages, gifts, meals, etc.

As your life goes on, remember that for suffering people, their lives will never be the same again. They may never be the same people they once were. Suffering and grief on this scale will change a person forever.

That year of firsts is particularly important. Even for the most unsentimental of people (like myself), it is difficult to ignore the pain that is felt on all of those first anniversaries without their loved one. Acknowledgment is such a powerful sign of love. If you want to be a friend to those who have suffered loss, the best thing you can do is show them you have not forgotten. Let them know that their loss is important to them, so it is important to you.

To anyone who is reading this who has suffered or continues to suffer on a deep, "dark night of the soul" level, if your life truly belongs to Jesus, fear not. You are in good, strong hands. He loses none that the father has given him (John 6:39). He will carry you through this time, and you can pour out your heart to him. He can handle your anger, your faithlessness, and your grief. Seek him with all of your heart, and be encouraged. Contemplate these tremendous verses from Lamentations 3:22–26:

> The steadfast love of the Lord never ceases; his mercies never come to an end; they are new every morning; great is your faithfulness. "The Lord is my portion," says my soul, "Therefore I will hope in him." The Lord is good to those who wait for him, to the soul who seeks him. It is good that one should wait quietly for the salvation of the Lord.

Just wait on him. Be at peace with waiting on him. He will restore you.

If you are somebody who does not know Jesus personally, but you want to, all you need to do is pray a sincere prayer in a quiet moment—even now—and ask Jesus to reveal himself to you personally, to forgive you for your sin, and to make you friends with God. You will not be made a fool of. Jesus answers a sincere prayer such as this *every* time. You will be amazed.

It has been my privilege to share these intimate and difficult moments of my life with you. I am blessed to be able to share Stephen's life and death with those who will listen, because it is nothing other than an immense testimony to God's grace and love in my life and in the lives of my family.

Epilogue

I still weep daily for the loss of my son. I will feel his absence for as long as I am on this earth, and more than ever before, my heart longs for the day when Christ will restore all things unto himself and set everything right. I have pain that will always be a part of me until that day, and my own pain has opened my eyes more and more to the suffering that is present in this world. More than ever, the cry of my heart is, "Come, Lord Jesus, come!"

But until then, I will rely on the Lord for my strength and my joy, for there is nothing and nowhere else in this world where I can obtain these things. Every good gift in this world that brings me joy is from God, and my cup truly runneth over.

I sit here in awe of how one little boy—one baby who doctors were so eager to dismiss—has changed my life and changed the lives of so many. He was such a little boy, yet he was the biggest display of God's glory, majesty, and grace I have ever experienced. What comfort it gives me to know that God can use even the smallest and most helpless of us for his magnificent purposes. Praise be to God!

On the day of Stephen's funeral, my sister handed me a piece of paper. She had lovingly taken the time to write down the ways in which Stephen's life had enriched her own. One of her final statements is a truth that has touched me deeply, and I wish to share it with you in closing.

> Of the forty-seven hours he lived outside of you, my sister, there were not many of those hours when he was not in the arms of someone who loved him utterly. There are not many people who can say they have been lovingly embraced for such a significant portion of their life.

Heavenly Father,

Thank you for the opportunity and the privilege of being Stephen's mother. Thank you for allowing me to know you more deeply through my suffering and that Stephen's life has not been in vain. Thank you for keeping all of your promises and that your Word stands firm. Thank you for the cross of Jesus and that Stephen is now walking and leaping in heaven with you. Thank you that because of your salvation, I too will someday stand before you and worship you face to face for the blessing of being all I am in you. In the meantime, may I honour you in all my thoughts, in all I do, and in all I say as your servant, as a wife, and as a mother to my other precious children. Praise and glory and honour and majesty to you forever! Amen!

i The American Heritage® Dictionary of the English Language, Fourth Edition copyright ©2000 by Houghton Mifflin Company. Updated in 2009. Published by Houghton Mifflin Company. All rights reserved

ii Lyrics are from 'My Hope Is Built', lyrics by Edward Mote, 1797-1874

iii Information has been gathered from articles published by The Medical Journal of Australia stating that although 12-15% of confirmed pregnancies end in miscarriage (Boyce, Condon & Ellwood 2002) that if very early pregnancies are also taken into consideration, that number is as high as 30% (McLaren & Shelley 2001). Sources:

Philip M Boyce, John T Condon and David A Ellwood (2002). Pregnancy loss: a major life event affecting emotional health and well-being. Retrieved March 02, 2012, from The Medical Journal of Australia: http://www.mja.com.au/public/issues/176_06_180302/boy10076.html

McLaren, B., & Shelley, J. M. (2002). Reported management of early-pregnancy bleeding and miscarriage by general practitioners in Victoria. Retrieved March 02, 2012, from The Medical Journal of Australia: http://www.mja.com.au/public/issues/176_02_210102/mcl10306_fm.html

iv James 1:19-20, Numbers 14:18, Psalm 103:8

v This was the information given to us verbally by the geneticists. I do not know the source of their information. However, medical research suggests that there is even less likelihood of live birth, with statistics ranging between 1:10,000 to 1:16,000 live births. Sources:

Redlinger-Grosse, K., Bernhardt, B. A., Berg, K., Muenke, M., & Biesecker, B. B. (2002). The Decision to Continue: The Experiences and Needs of Parents Who Receive a Prenatal Diagnosis of Holoprosencephaly. *American Journal of Medical Genetics* , 112:369-378.

Pineda-Alvarez, D. E., Dubourg, C., David, V., Roessler, E., & Muenke, M. (Unknown). Retrieved March 12, 2012, from Inria: Current Recommendations for the molecular evaluation of newly diagnosed holoprosencephaly patients. Am J Med Genet C Semin Med Genet.http://hal.inria.fr/docs/00/46/20/36/PDF/inserm-00462036_edited.pdf

Dubourg C, Bendavid C, Pasquier L, henry C, Odent S, David V. (2007). Holoprosencephaly. Orphanet J Rare Dis. 2:2:8

vi Taken from John Piper's Facebook status update January 21,2012

vii The statistic of a 1 in 200 possibility of miscarriage was the information given to us verbally by the medical staff treating us. Upon further investigation, I can find no definitive proof that having an amniocentesis increases the risk of miscarriage. The 1 in 200 statistic appears to be accurate, but that doesn't change from those who have and those who haven't had the test. The websites supporting this view include The Royal Women's Hospital (www.thewomens.org.au/amniocentesis) and Melbourne Radiology (site needed). The Victorian Government's Better Health website: (www.betterhealth.vic.gov.au/bhcv2/bhcarticles.nsf/pages/Amniocentesis) states less than 1% of women who undergo the test suffer a "spontaneous abortion" and that not all of these miscarriages are related to the test. Consequently, the 1 in 200 statistic given to us seems to be accurate, but could be misleading.

[viii] It is difficult to find statistics about full term stillborns as the term "stillborn" is applied to any baby that dies in utero or during birth after 20 weeks gestation or over 400g birth weight (if gestation is unknown). In Australia and New Zealand, stillbirth is the death of a baby before or during birth, from the 20th week of pregnancy onwards, or 400 grams birth weight. 2008 statistics show that in Australia and New Zealand 1 in every 130-135 women giving birth will have a still born child of 20 weeks gestation or more. The majority of stillbirths are normally formed babies that die at or beyond 28 weeks gestation where, if born alive at that gestation, survival approaches 100%. Over the last 10 years the number of stillbirths in Australia has remained steady, with approximately 2000 stillbirths each year.

Sources:

Australia and New Zealand Fact Sheet: Stillbirth. Retrieved March 02, 2012, from Australian and New Zealand Stillbirth Alliance:

http://www.sidsandkids.org/wp-content/uploads/Lancet_launch_ANZSA_Factsheet.pdf

Stillbirth Foundation Australia. Stillbirth in Australia. http://www.stillbirthfoundation.org.au/sbf/Stillbirth%20in%20Australia%20website%20version.pdf

[ix] Marshall, I. H., Millard, A. R., Packer, J. I., & Wiseman, D. J. (Eds.). (1996). *New Bible Dictionary* (3 ed.). Leicester, England: Inter-Varsity Press. Used with permission.

[x] www.familiesforhope.org

[xi] At the time, I had misinterpreted the medical research I had undertaken. Yet, having undertaken further research since, we have found that 50% of babies born with Alobar Holoprosencephaly will survive birth and live anywhere up to 6 days, and a 38% chance that babies will survive anywhere up to 2.6 years of age. This is still a long way from the 99.9% 'statistic' we were repeatedly told. Sources:

Olsen C, Hughes, JP, Younglood LG, Sharpe-Stimac M. (1997). Epidemiology of holoprosencephaly and phenotypic characteristics of affected children. Am J Med Genet 73:217-226

Redlinger-Grosse, K., Bernhardt, B. A., Berg, K., Muenke, M., & Biesecker, B. B. (2002). The Decision to Continue: The Experiences and Needs of Parents Who Receive a Prenatal Diagnosis of Holoprosencephaly. *American Journal of Medical Genetics*, 112:369-378.

[xii] Piper, J. (2011, May 21). *Why Was This Child Born Blind?* Retrieved March 2, 2012, from desiringGod: http://www.desiringgod.org/resource-library/sermons/why-was-this-child-born-blind By John Piper. © Desiring God. Used with permission.

[xiii] MacArthur, J. (2012). *God: Is He? Who Is He?* Retrieved March 2, 2012, from Grace To You: http://www.gty.org/resources/print/sermons/1351 Copyright ©2012 Grace to You

[xiv] Piper, J. (2011, May 21). *Why Was This Child Born Blind?* Retrieved March 2, 2012, from desiringGod: http://www.desiringgod.org/resource-library/sermons/why-was-this-child-born-blind By John Piper. © Desiring God. Used with permission.

[xv] Robson, S. J., Tan, W. S., Adeyemi, A., & Dear, K. B. (2009, September 8). *Birth: Issues in Prenatal Care.* Retrieved March 12, 2012, from Wiley Online Library: http://onlinelibrary.wiley.com/doi/10.1111/j.1523-536X.2009.00331.x/abstract.

[xvi] Refer to endnote xi.

[xvii] Paterson, C. (2011). *Love, Tears & Autism.* Mona Vale: Ark House Press. Used with permission.

[xviii] Taken from "He'll Take Care of the Rest" by Keith Green

[xix] http://www.fathersloveletter.com/

[xx] http://www.bearsofhope.org.au/a/134.html

[xxi] Lyrics by John Newton.

[xxii] Wright, NT (1997). *For All God's Worth: True Worship and the Calling of the Church*: Wm. B. Eerdmans Publishing Co.

www.ingramcontent.com/pod-product-compliance
Lightning Source LLC
Chambersburg PA
CBHW051758040426
42446CB00007B/420